Fighting Will

Luke Chichetto

Copyright © 2017 Luke Chichetto

All rights reserved. In accordance with U.S. Copyright Act of 1976, the scanning, uploading, and electronic sharing of any part of this book without permission of the publisher constitute unlawful piracy and theft of the author's intellectual property. No part of this book may be reproduced in any form by any electronic or mechanical means (including photocopying, recording or information storage and retrieval) without permission in writing from the author or publisher. Thank you for your support of the author's rights. If you would like to buy wholesale copies for libraries or bookstores, please contact the publisher at 727-940-7647

Published by Richter Publishing LLC www.richterpublishing.com

Book Cover Design: Luke Chichetto and Jessie Alarcon

Editors: Mandi Weems, Erica Susan Garvin, Emma Kilkelly, Kati Scanlon & Katharina Jung

Additional Contributors: Amanda Jean Dalugdug

Library of Congress Cataloging-in-Publication Data in process

ISBN: 10:1-945812-17-6

ISBN-13: 978-1-945812-17-0

DISCLAIMER

This book is designed to provide information on life, sports & spirituality only. This information is provided and sold with the knowledge that the publisher and author do not offer any legal or medical advice. In the case of a need for any such expertise consult with the appropriate professional. This book does not contain all information available on the subject. This book has not been created to be specific to any individual people or organizations' situation or needs. Reasonable efforts have been made to make this book as accurate as possible. However, there may be typographical and or content errors. Therefore, this book should serve only as a general guide and not as the ultimate source of subject information. This book contains information that might be dated or erroneous and is intended only to educate and entertain. The author and publisher shall have no liability or responsibility to any person or entity regarding any loss or damage incurred, or alleged to have incurred, directly or indirectly, by the information contained in this book or as a result of anyone acting or failing to act upon the information in this book. You hereby agree never to sue and to hold the author and publisher harmless from any and all claims arising out of the information contained in this book. You hereby agree to be bound by this disclaimer, covenant not to sue and release. You may return this book within the guarantee time period for a full refund. In the interest of full disclosure, this book contains affiliate links that might pay the author or publisher a commission upon any purchase from the company. While the author and publisher take no responsibility for any virus or technical issues that could be caused by such links, the business practices of these companies and or the performance of any product or service, the author or publisher has used the product or service and makes a recommendation in good faith based on that experience. All characters appearing in this work are fictitious. Any resemblance to real persons, living or dead is purely coincidental. The views in the book are that solely of the author and not of the publisher. All block quotes have been sampled from the Tao Te Ching by Lao-tzu or Wayne Dyer and they own the rights to that information. The writings and views of this book are of the author and not of the publisher.

DEDICATION

I would like to dedicate this to the three children that I'm raising. My daughters: Lilliana, Daniella and Cassandra; they are my life. I want to see them be able to experience the growth that I went through and learn to enjoy life and be their true selves. So, it means a lot to me to present this memoir to the three people in my life that mean so much to me.

All under heaven have a common beginning
This beginning is the Mother of the world
Having known the Mother,
we may proceed to know her children
Having known the children,
we should go back and hold on to the Mother

CONTENTS

DEDICATION v

ACKNOWLEDGMENTS 7

INTRODUCTION 11

CHAPTER 1: WHAT IS LIFE? 27

CHAPTER 2: ELEMENTARY AND MIDDLE SCHOOL 31

CHAPTER 3: HIGH SCHOOL 44

CHAPTER 4: AFTER HIGH SCHOOL 62

CHAPTER 5: ITALY 77

CHAPTER 6: AFTER ITALY 85

CHAPTER 7: STARTING A BUSINESS 95

CHAPTER 8: ARIZONA 107

CHAPTER 9: NFL 124

Chapter 10: MOBILITY RX 138

Chapter 11: INVENTION 144

CHAPTER 12: I AM 149

ACKNOWLEDGMENTS

I would like to acknowledge my wife, Denise. She has been a big part of my life. Eleven years of marriage and counting. Through all of the struggles I faced, she has been my biggest supporter. I love her for everything she's done. I think a lot of times it can be challenging for both the person going through difficult times, but it also affects the spouse and friends. It doesn't matter what the challenge is, whether it is anxiety or depression. Regardless of what I was going through, Denise never gave up on me.

I'd also like to thank the author Wayne Dyer. His perspectives and writings enabled me to think differently about life. The effect his writing had on me ran hand in hand with Denise; where she had one part of me and Wayne Dyer had the other. In the early stages of finding my true identity, I cried and thought I would lose her; based on the paradigms that I was stuck in. "Despite my internal struggles and insecurities as that I experienced during this stage of my life, Denise stayed loyal in her support of me.

The first book of Dyer's I read was *Wishes Fulfilled*. There was a segment in there that really opened me up and for me it was like drinking new Kool-Aid. I wanted Denise to read Dyer's book. Denise told me she might not understand those exact words, but she supported me. I now own 15 Wayne Dyer books. So, there's a parallel there; both Denise and Dyer have been my key to finding the truth.

Fighting Will

HEAVEN IS ETERNAL - THE EARTH ENDURES
WHY DO HEAVEN AND EARTH LAST FOREVER?
THEY DO NOT LIVE FOR THEMSELVES ONLY
THIS IS THE SECRET OF THEIR DURABILITY.

FOR THIS REASON THE SAGE PUTS HIMSELF LAST
AND SO ENDS UP AHEAD
HE STAYS A WITNESS TO LIFE
SO ENDURES.

SERVE THE NEEDS OF OTHERS,
AND ALL YOUR OWN NEEDS WILL BE FULFILLED
THROUGH SELFLESS ACTION, FULFILLMENT IS
ATTAINED.

-7th Verse of the Tao Te Ching by Lao-tzu

INTRODUCTION

I entered this world a little over 10lbs on March 14th, 1980. Born in Massachusetts as Luke Edward Chichetto, I am the fourth child of the family, with my brothers Mark, Peter, and John ahead of me. I am not sure where the name Luke came from except maybe from the Bible, but I know Edward came from my maternal grandfather, Edward Callahan, a Korean War Veteran who died in that forgotten and tragic war. The vibes to leave must have been strong when I was born because we only lived there four years. After the decision to move due to various family circumstances was made, we relocated to Winter Haven, Florida in 1984.

One of the key concepts that has been central to my life is Wayne Dyer's concept of about Edging God Out, or EGO. Through EGO, you are edging out a concept of God, a spirit, or source and then following the memories of what feels like a true-self. This will be explored in depth in subsequent chapters

As early as my mind will let me remember, I have gone through life with an EGO of sorts. It seems that I have also been hitched to a hungry, knowledge-driven, over-filled mind. God or the concept of God had to be more than what I was taught it was when I was little. That concept seemed too limited, too narrow. If wonder is the basis of worship, my wonder of all the complications around me seemed too gig for a small God, a limited divinity. I wanted more, something greater to sustain me when I tried to make sense of things. In addition to this, having older brothers has put that mind and ego on a fast lane of sorts, always moving fast-forward to keep up with them. The down side of this fraternal pace and competition was that I wanted to be more clever and smarter for them, so to speak, and for their need instead of for myself and my own needs. That sounds crazy to some people, but it is what it is in my memory.

To date, my soul is still trying to slow down. It is also trying to think of myself and of my own quest than just wanting to be clever and wise for my brothers' sake and for others. They say you have to love your neighbor as yourself, but first you have to love yourself, respect yourself and inner needs. With so many interesting things happening on the planet and in our growing planet-consciousness through the internet, it is hard not to want more and to want to grow within, right? So balance is necessary, to bring into proportion my inner and outer needs. But overall, I need to slow down, smell the roses, and look at the things and people around me, especially with Denise and our three beautiful girls. I need also to learn to give to others in the same measure as I have received from others, whether from the living or the dead.

As a baby, we grow up with this "give me more" attitude. It is no one's fault. It seems we are born into this kind of environment. I was given a name, was cared for with good food, water, clothing, toys, and a wonderful upbringing. By most accounts, I was fortunate. I played sports, went to school, met wonderful people in my life and continue to.

The one problem or challenge to all this is that I also took on an ego and groomed it during this time of growth and development, sometimes by choice, sometimes because of the influence of others.

I want to let everyone who reads this understand that at one time my heart, mind, and consciousness felt completed and satisfied, but not my ego. Why did my ego not feel complete?

It is hard to deny that I have an ego, especially writing this book and telling my story. Let me try to explain why I am writing this book about my life, my ego and also about trying to "edge God out," so to speak, a saying I borrowed from writer, Wayne Dyer

I grew up Catholic, so God to me at that time was this God whom I said prayers to every day or in times of desperate need. It was as if I was up with God in a spaceship of sorts or on the cusp of his eternal awareness; with God looking over the universe as if we were like ants. I lived like this for many years. I was part of an awareness of God and God was part of an awareness of me. Because I lived with this personal image of God, my ego grew quite large, almost cosmic.

I am not trying to bash Christianity, the Catholic Church, or other religions. I am just stating how I felt and what I believed at the time. We learn from the senses, and this is what I sensed at the time. All religion interpreted or examined according to one's experience, and personal knowledge is different. My experience of Christianity through Catholicism led me to imagine God like a dictator and imagine myself linked up to this God in my ego and consciousness.

Ego can be anything we label like color, race, sex, big, small, poor, rich, and so much more, including stories like the ones I read from childhood. Ego can be anything we think and want it to be.

I like to think of Einstein's theory of relativity for example. The theory suggests that it does not matter what one thinks if it's relative to the person and it makes sense to him or her. How one discovers the insight is all that matters to the ego.

As the youngest, I was often spoiled. Despite this, I was still able to develop a strong work ethic through competition with my older brothers as I proved I was worthy of their respect. As I tried to keep up with my growing ego, I learned and absorbed whatever I could. I played baseball and football. I knew that if I could show my family that I was able to achieve, then I could gain their trust. On the flip side, I was also exposed to a lot at a young age. This exposure often included movies, magazines, drinking, smoking, and vandalizing. At this point I was at a unique stage of my life, where I sometimes behaved like a child, and at other times, an adult. I was learning how to steal, manipulate people, and hurt others through fights. My ego was downloading quickly like a ipod plugged into the worlds thoughts. I had a bigoted view of homosexuality and judgmental of other things. I was even opinionated about money and the lack-there-of.

My mother was a stay home mom until I was 10 years old. My father worked as a school teacher. He went to law school and loved what he did, so he was a major proponent of a quality education. My parents were both a huge influence on me with their love, kindness, and want always to do the right thing. But what exactly is the right thing?

As a kid, I did not understand this and still do because it is still man made words. I only wanted to have fun. So, going out learning from other people and arguing my way through life was a major part of my ego. It seemed I looked at everyone as wrong, especially if they disagreed with me. I often reasoned: HOW COULD I BE WRONG? Again these are thoughts. I am sure immigrants, students, police on duty, doctors prescribing meds, terrorists, soldiers, and parents all ask the same questions: WHAT IS RIGHT? WHAT IS WRONG? Did the terrorists in Brussels and Berlin ask these questions? I am sure they did to the horror of the world To elaborate, an example is if a bad man waters a plant it grows, but if a good man doesn't, the plant dies. It is the right thing to give the plant fluids, and the plant doesn't care who is actually taking care of it., as it with thrive the same.

Another example: if Robin Hood steals from the rich and gives to the poor is he good? One perception is that he's a thief and the other is he's righteous for helping out the less fortunate.

Having brothers, I managed to have my share of altercations. I remember having my first fist fight at the age of four. My brothers watched me fight until they intervened. This ego mind, or downloaded mind, was the start of a very hard life. My ego made me very aggressive and gave me a lot of ups and downs to contend with in my early days. I became selfish, argumentative, and spoiled. Although I experienced some happiness, I also felt a lot of grief because I always had the need to prove myself. I had to be right all the time.

I write of this to let everyone know that ego-centeredness sabotages life. Such an ego impairs, damages, and subverts what is best in a person. It also disables all that is potentially good and life-giving in a person. Not surprisingly, I fought kids in elementary school and middle school. I even got expelled from middle school for fighting, and my father had to go to a school hearing in order to get me accepted back in.

I am grateful to have overcome this addictive behavior. I can tell you that it was not until I hit high school that I stopped starting so many fights. In high school,
I started to play sports and got interested in girls. I never had to make trouble. I matured and started to see how life around older aged kids with scratchy cars acted. I soon learned my role, and eventually took on a new EGO. I wanted to get into shape, play football, and be popular. EGO is funny. It wants all of it and more.

Ever wonder why we are given a dictionary and told to write out words and we learn to spell in school? The same is true with math. We are given a text and told to learn addition and subtraction. What was the point? It has to do with EGO. This is the same EGO that I have and that you have, that makes up the rules and then when these rules do not fit our make-up, we change them. Or society does. That is, the rules of grammar, language, and science can bend to make them work for us, for our welfare.

In life, we make up certain rules in our minds or download rules from other sources from society, science, religion, law, or even the environment. This is so that our beliefs, which keep things together, make life livable. These beliefs or practices also give an order to society. Think of hospital rules, traffic rules, and rules of behavior for marriage and laws that protect society, especially the young All of these attempt to control people, especially wayward people, potential criminals, from doing harm. Yet they are all manmade rules, passed down to us, that eventually get into our sub-conscience and become second nature. At least we hope they do, especially laws and codes regarding our safety and survival.

> When the greatness of the Tao is present,
> action arises from one's own heart.
> When the greatness of the Tao is absent,
> action comes from the rules
> of "kindess and justice".
>
> If you need rules to be kind and just,
> if you act virtuous,
> this is a surge sign that virtue is absent.
> This we see they great hypocrisy.
>
> When kinship falls into discord,
> piety and ritesof devotion arise.
> When the country falls into chaso,
> official loyalists will appear,
> patriotism is born.
>
> -18th Verse of the Tao Te Ching by Lao-tzu

Former professor of medicine at Stanford University, Dr Bruce Lipton "most of our decisions, actions, emotions and behavior depend on the 95% of brain activity that is beyond our conscious awareness, which means that 95 – 99% of our life comes from the programming in our subconscious mind".So all the work we do in schools, whether in high school, medical school, technical school, or any other type of school is just filling the mind with what other EGOs want you to know or do. This knowledge can become addictive and potentially dangerous. The more we let others teach us without ever allowing our minds to contemplate the "why?", the more we become controlled by the wrong sources. We always need to know the "why?". For example, when I go to a doctor for a prescription, I need to know why he or she is providing me with the prescription. If I don't know why, then I can become addicted, using medication repeatedly. We should be aware of the "why?" about all things we put into ourselves, whether food or medication, so that we can take care of our body and mind.

Ever wonder why we fear some things and not of others? It's due to the way we were taught and brought up. We were told what to do, what to avoid, and what not to do. We sub-consciously took all these rules and customs into our heads and memorized them. They became part of our behavior.

I can remember some scary movies I watched as a kid that were downloaded in my mind and stayed with me, within my subconscious, to the point of needing to stay in my parents' bedroom at night to sleep. These horrible images and feelings lasted until I was 12 years old.

My EGO said, 'why are you wasting this time worrying? You are a fool.' That's the point, right? Why waste time worrying about a film or movie that is just contrived to make a kid freak out or be terrified. My EGO must learn to control these outer fears.

As a result of struggling and wrestling with these fears and aggressions, and overcoming them, I can say today that I am God/Source or son of God, as the Psalms say, and say it with excitement, based on a deeper understanding of who I am and where I am going in life. I can also say this because I am not fearful or aggressive any more. I am open to others, to listen to them, and to dialogue. We are all one and should aim for solidarity with all people, regardless of race, color, creed, or background.

I want to tell you this so I can continue to write and not bore you with all my experiences that a lot of the world is experiencing. I just know that if you have ever communed with yourself, meditated upon who you are and what inner powers you possess, you will feel the same as me. Such inner reflection – talking to your inner life -- gives you inner knowledge. Buddha speaks of this inner self as does Jesus when the latter says the kingdom of God is within a person, not out there in space. Go into the soul, the soul's inner space, he is saying. Like history, it is infinite. Search for soul food, to nourish your life, your existence. If the mind works like a dictionary or computer, telling you what is right or wrong, the soul, the interior part of us, works like an inner ocean, buoying up the mind and sustaining the whole person -- all a person's emotions, feeling and thoughts -- in an infinite motion of mystery and wonder, wave after wave of it. This is why getting in touch with this inner self, and staying with it, makes life so much more exciting and rewarding.

What you look at or hear – have you ever wondered why? Why anything? Have you ever wondered -- Who am I? Are you the kid, the infant, or the adult? And where are you in your mind, in your life, in your career? What do you thing about thinking? Where does language come from, for example? Infants seem to learn it quickly. Why? What we feel and see and touch and taste comes from somewhere outside us and inside us. We don't live in a vacuum. We are the product of millions of years and thousands of generations before us. We are the products of our ancestors. Do you wonder about questions of inequality? Why some have all and some have very little in society? What about greed, hate, grievances, between Muslims and Jews, Buddhists and Muslims, Christians and Muslims? What about climate change? Why do you even consider these questions or read this? Maybe you are searching for answers? What called you to the store to buy this? What is keeping you to stay with this page, this book? Why do you keep reading it?

Well if you have the answer to all these questions, then please let me know. I have asked all these questions and they have driven me to a very low place. I did not want to live, at one time. Sound like anyone else?

Probably not, right? Probably not right to think that way? Does it sound like you? Maybe not! We all come from different backgrounds and have different resources, social and spiritual, to cope with things. And we all have different experiences.

I can say, however, that this thing I call EGO wants to do right, the right thing. As I stated earlier, edging God out or and old, outdated concept of God, is necessary.

Ever wonder why your body heals itself when you leave it alone – like a cut or broken arm? What do you believe in? Medicine or do you act like a Christian Scientist, who does not believe in any medicine, just natural healing through prayer?

Why do you feel the wind on your body? You know it exists because of the way the branches bend and the hairs on your head move when it invisibly blows on them. You can't see the wind except through the movement of things around it.

Ever wonder why your fingernails grow or why your hair does? There are too many things to list for now, no?

Well, this is what happens to me, as times. I have all these questions hitting me at once. I have been going through my life and thinking I knew everything and that I was right about everything. Then one fine day my wife and I were on a plane and my body could not keep up with all of this – all of the questions, unanswered thoughts, and mysteries surrounding me. I had a panic attack or something like that from an overload of stress. While on the plane, my mind crashed in the clouds, so to speak, caved in, froze. I was motionless.

My mind or EGO mind wants to know everything and it was being beaten up, so to speak. I was losing all my certainties. I was becoming vulnerable, but it was the best thing that could have happened to me. I had to retrain my brain, tame it, to think differently, to think on my own because I had become fearful of everything and no one outside of this body of mine could help me at the time.

Some of the inner fear I was experiencing at the time made me want to do nothing more, just give up. I thought I was alone thinking this, too. I thought: how could a athlete of 230 pounds, active in high school and college football, used to kicking ass, be so scared of life?

I talked to councilors, all kinds of them. I took drugs to help my body function and make it feel good.

But what is good, right???? My life is filled with other peoples' EGOS of what is good or bad for me. How was I to come out of this hell I had gotten myself into? I wanted to climb out of it not go further down into its darkness.

I found myself talking to myself, calling for help, self-help, and help started to slowly surface from within me. Is there any other explanation for this? No, I prayed and prayed to myself. Where your treasure is, there will your heart also be, I thought.

As each of us start looking for answers like a dog digging for his or her bone until he or she find it or like a miner looking for gold – we find a way out of our hollow space, our confusion, our inner darkness. Somehow we manage. In my situation, meditation got me through, out of my hole or darkness, my sunless self.

Call it God/ Source or Higher Power? Tao or anything you want! Again, the mystery is just a name you assign to it, but it was for me just a clean knowing. It provided me with a new start and put me on a long road of self-discovery and learning.

For the first time in my life I felt connected with words, words and sounds talking back to me in my head that made sense. It went from silence, to sound to words to language to sense, in one wave of thought after another. Wow! What a feeling!

I think we are as divine as God or one's concept of God. In the book, *The Chronicles of Narnia,* the character Eustace is surprised to find a star is an actual intelligent being and says: "I thought a star was just burning gasses." The star answers: "That is what I am made of – not what a star is."

That's how I feel now. I am not just what people say I am or how they have labeled me. I am unique and a mystery. I am not just carbon, oxygen, hydrogen, and nitrogen. I am more, so much more. Unlike a star, I have a consciousness, a consciousness that can reflect on it all.

Great leaders like Jesus and Buddha want us to open up to a world of consciousness on a different plane; or on many planes, not just a cerebral one. The plane of consciousness and of the subconscious, and simple everyday awareness, puts us on a threshold of wonder and newness.

I think I have started that journey and what surprises me is that I have put myself on that journey. Little did I realize that the ride in the sky would lead me to a deeper ride and journey into my own realm of wonder and mystery; opening up each day in my soul and in the people around me.

Growing up with that mentality and then going through a stage of life that was daunting caused me to become depressed and have anxiety. I suddenly didn't want to live anymore, and I wanted to take my own life. This incident caused me to see life for what it was; it was the biggest learning curve.

At the age of seven, I worked for the Boston Red Sox as a bat boy. Sports have been the one constant in my life, I always enjoyed playing them, through childhood and even when I grew up and moved away from my family.

Growing up with three older brothers, we all played sports. Playing baseball was what I fell in love with, but I also played football and at the collegiate level too. It was my love of sports that started my deep desire to be in the sports industry. It drove me into several jobs, which went from internships to paid, full-time positions.

My first big job was with the University of South Florida as an intern strength coach. From there, I opened my own little gym, but I still wasn't fulfilled. So, I went back to sports. I worked with the Texas Rangers for five years and then I worked with Tampa Bay Buccaneers. Sports have played a big role in my life and taught me many great lessons.

I would say the biggest thing to realize in life is that everybody is the same—whether you're a professional athlete or you're working in a Laundromat. Everyone has the same potential to discover their true identity.

It is easy to become someone based on how we are defined according to how society labels us. I can see that clearly now that I've overcome so many challenges in life. I see people that come into Mobility Rx, the gym I now own, that are all different types and sizes yet they have similar problems; they come looking for help with there body. Its hard not to become close and friends because I ask how they are doing and become a psychologist. Sometimes they shed tears warming up on the bike, and they open up just like I did.

I want this book to show you that it's okay to open up. It's perfectly fine to take time in order to figure out who you are. I want you to see that everything is completely up to you.

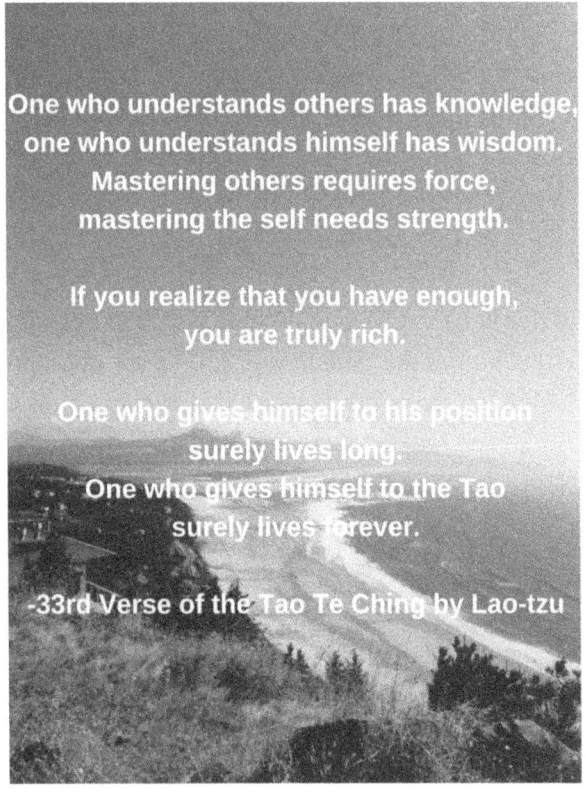

One who understands others has knowledge,
one who understands himself has wisdom.
Mastering others requires force,
mastering the self needs strength.

If you realize that you have enough,
you are truly rich.

One who gives himself to his position
surely lives long.
One who gives himself to the Tao
surely lives forever.

-33rd Verse of the Tao Te Ching by Lao-tzu

CHAPTER 1: WHAT IS LIFE?

When I think of my childhood and everything I did as a kid, I know that I never sat down and just thought: *what is life*? I'm sure that no adolescent thinks about this concept like we do when we are adults.

I want you to stop and think about that: what is life?

It's a makeup of what you want, what you are, what you do, and what your familiarities are. Everyone's experiences are different, so no two people will ever undergo the same events. When you think back on your life events, they will really stand out, especially those moments that you can see changed you in a significant way.

The biggest things that jump out when I think about "what life is?" were things I did as a child. Now at 36, I can look back in retrospect and think "why did I do that?" or "I did that because I was taught to." You may not have been brought up like me, but you will have your own set of unique experiences, beliefs, and teachings that will have shaped your way of thinking.

Once you start to question your way of thinking, you begin to wonder what other people think about and how they define their 'truth.' It's then that you really start to question yourself and your beliefs. This method of questioning brings you around to really ponder what 'truth' actually is to you. You try to remember when you started to become your true self or when you realized what beliefs in your life were still worth keeping.

The biggest part of questioning myself and my definition of life came when I started to reminisce about my childhood. Growing up with three older brothers, we had our share of ups and downs. I thought about all the sports that I played: baseball, football, soccer, and so on. Playing sports had a significant impact on what I did and how I did it.

I have wonderful parents who are still supportive of everything I do. They greatly influenced me to do certain things in life. I have questioned what their impact means to me and my life overall. Because my parents only know from their own experiences in life, they raised me based on their accumulated knowledge. So, in realizing all of that, I am better prepared for now. I have three daughters of my own, and I try not to tell them what life is.

Everyone has at least one person that they look up to or look to for advice (parents, siblings, teachers, and friends, and others throughout their entire life). You ask questions, try to learn from others, and watch how others react to different situations. We all do this until the point where you finally figure out your own life.

For me, it took hitting rock bottom to finally figure that out. And not everybody experiences rock bottom to figure out their meaning of life. On your own, you finally realize to *live* is life. That's the beauty of it.

If you look at present day things and how they affect your life and those around you, you will start to see it. For example, I watch *Sesame Street* with my girls. They see the monsters, and they'll say, "Show me your sad face," and I show a sad face. Next, they'll ask me to show a happy face; then I show a happy face. It makes you wonder if that is life? Just mimicking what everyone else does, says, and feels? Too many times we simply go along with that idea because we don't know to question things…yet.

Another example of the girls' learning was when we went to a bonfire at a friend's house. They walked up to the fire, and they could feel that it was hot. They didn't get any closer. I didn't need to teach them they were going to burn themselves if they got too close. Now, when they ask what a blaze is, I can give them information based on how the term is defined. However, learning that fire is hot and will burn them is more of an automatic and instinctive learning process.

Nevertheless, we keep questioning life. We do not just learn because somebody is teaching us what life is. Instead, we need to expand our inner being, and just let life be.
This is really what I want people to realize. So many times,

we find ourselves stuck in a definition. We have an egotistical mindset that's saying this is how it is. This is why there are still countless countries at war right now. They are fighting over what life might be. They even fight over being religion. The biggest thing I'm trying to convey is that everyone should start questioning ingrained beliefs and predetermined definitions of life.

> A truly good man is not aware of his goodness
> and is therefore good.
> A foolish man tries to be good
> and is therefore not good.
>
> The master does nothing,
> yet he leaves nothing undone.
> The ordinary man is always doing things,
> yet many more are left to be done.
>
> The highest virtue is to act without a sense of self.
> The highest kindness is to give without condition.
> The highest justice is to see without preference.
>
> The great master follows his own nature
> and not the trappings of life.
>
> -38th Verse of the Tao Te Ching by Lao-tzu

CHAPTER 2: ELEMENTARY AND MIDDLE SCHOOL

Growing up was a memorable experience. Of course, I have a different perspective on it now, since I don't try to label it so much. In order to tell you what my beliefs were, I have to share my experience of being the youngest of my brothers.

My dad was working full-time, and my mom was a stay-at-home mom. I was about ten years old when she went back to nursing. Throughout my younger years, I was seen as just the baby. I was favored by my mom, and I felt as though I was looked down upon by my brothers. I was always battling and in competition with life and my older brothers. I felt that I always had to excel. That I needed to have a work ethic with a strong drive. All of these thoughts came from being the youngest brother and being put on a pedestal by my mom.

In retrospect, I did many things at a young age that other kids weren't able to do. With time, I hung out more with friends and less and less with my brothers. However, my brother John and I hung out together more because we shared a room. John and I are sixteen months apart, which is closer in age than I am to my oldest brothers: Mark and Peter. Mark is seven years older than me, and Peter is five years older. For the most part, like many families, we all pretty much hung out since we were together a lot. I think that Mark and I clashed a lot just due to the large age difference. With Mark being the first child, there was more of an emphasis on what was expected of him than what was expected of me. So, there was an underlying jealousy between us. I still notice it even to this day, but it isn't nearly to the same degree that is used to be.

I would say that my younger years were heavily influenced by my brothers. I saw things at a younger age that I wouldn't have if my family dynamic was different. I'm saying this from a moral standpoint, but not as an attitude of good or bad. In society's eyes, I would say that I should not have been seeing things that my oldest brother did, such as pornographic magazines or horror movies. I was still seven years younger than them. I also think that this exposure created a certain path in my mind that caught up with me later on.

I also had certain feelings of jealousy, because we had an older brother who was going out to parties and was in high school. I saw it like he's doing all these great things and I am not. We were always looking to see what our older brother was doing, whereas others didn't.

Sometimes, life was difficult as the youngest because I

was trying to earn respect from the other three. It didn't help that I was babied by mom. The fights came and went between us, if I didn't get my way, I would let them know. My willpower and ego kicked in at an early age. That and the stubbornness of course, which is defined as a type-A personality. Unfortunately, I didn't learn about this until I was older.

I always had my share of fights in school. It was a tough road for me. It even got to the point that I was expelled from middle school. I had gotten into many fights and made many mistakes. Again, this goes back to the introduction: *what was the truth that I was fighting for*? During my childhood, fighting everyone was what life was; it was my truth. I had to stick it out for my well-being.

I had this unbelievable thought at the time that since I was a pudgy kid and other kids called me fat, the name calling wasn't acceptable. I was going to stand up for myself and fight them. When I look back now, it is hard to explain what it felt like. I was being picked on a lot. It wasn't that they disagreed with my point of view. It was simply my belief that it was wrong to make fun of people.

You see, my parents did a wonderful job of raising us even though we weren't the wealthiest. Middle class is about where we fit in. There was a time when I had wonderful friends that were from all parts of the financial spectrum. Having a wide base of friends allowed me to see that in every area of society you want certain things in life. For example, if somebody's wearing a pair of Nikes that you want and you go home and say, "Mom, I want to get these." If your mom replies, "No, because we have to buy pizza tonight," this gives kids an awareness of financial constraints. Parents can't buy you a pair of shoes every time you want them. And I think that because of that I had a lot of animosity and spoiled tendencies.

Don't get me wrong, my brothers and I would get things that we wanted. We were never without. We always had shoes, we always had clothes, and we always ate good food. Sometimes we had eggs for dinner with pancakes; things that make kids happy. My mom made best the dinner, and that's what we knew. I don't think we were ever deprived in that way because we didn't know the difference. Mom always made dinners because she was a stay-at-home mom. She would always make a wonderful meal like shepherd's pie or rice casseroles. She always made something amazing, and we had no idea how she pulled it off every night. But there were times I thought that I should have something that my older brother had. That's what society calls "complex" because I'd show my spoiled tendencies.

At school, I had that same mentality. It was a little different because I was actually dealing with people who weren't my brothers. They would fight me back. Going about life in that way, you'll learn really quickly. Some people will think that it was due to pent-up anger or because I couldn't control the other kid.

However, I think this probably turned into more of an ego issue. It was "you-can't-whip-my-ass" type of mindset. The anger was there. I built the anger based around being around three older brothers, thinking that was the only way to live. This is why it's so important what we tell younger kids. This is what I am trying to do with my three daughters; the importance behind all this is about 'what is truth?'

The whole idea is to live life and not put a label based on what we should or shouldn't have. Growing up, anger was my life, and it escalated. Thanks to moral support from my father and mother, I was able to squash and maintain it. Nonetheless, it was still a part of me that wanted to come out. It was all relative to the egotistical mindset. It was the idea that if I couldn't get what I wanted as a spoiled kid, that I was going to fight for it. No matter what it was, I wasn't going to stop until I got it. I had an entitlement mentality.

I grew up Catholic and went to a Catholic school that was extremely strict. I made it all the way to the third grade before they pulled me out because I was, as they stated, "insubordinate." I wouldn't do what they wanted me to do. My mother was a substitute teacher for kindergarten one year and even laughed about this. She couldn't do it because I saw her as my mother-slash-substitute teacher. She would tell me to go to the office because I did not want to take a nap and acted out. She chased me around the classroom, then had to call down to the office to get me out of her classroom.

I wasn't the best academically either. I struggled due to the spoiled attitude and simply because I didn't want to go to school. I only wanted to go when I wanted to go. My terms, my time, and I certainly didn't want to listen to teachers. At the Catholic School, they did all kinds of little studies. They were trying to figure out what the hell was going on because I had problems with every little thing. My issues came simply from the fact I didn't like it. They ended up putting me into remedial classes. I excelled in all the other classes besides reading and writing. I probably could have aced a lot of things, but because I was being told how to do it, I didn't want to do it.

That starts to raise the issue again, of *what is truth*? And so, you start to consider the upbringing of the teachers and how they're presenting their truth in life. They say, "Wow, you must have a problem because all the other students are doing this and you are the only one not doing it. So, you have to get help." So that's what they did; they put me in classes that were taught by a remedial reading specialist.

I didn't put my head in the sand after that, but those classes were derived from the idea that I was not capable. I thought in my mind, *I just didn't want to do it*, and therefore I was slow or behind. I did get held back in second grade because of this mentality. That was a decision that my parents and teachers all thought was best for me. Ms. Hummer was the name of my second-grade teacher. She was great and was awfully kind to me. She really took a liking to me, and for the first time in a long time, I didn't really feel that need to rebel against her or what she was trying to teach me. Then it was time to move on to third grade. I had a little lapse in my anger because I wanted to be with Ms. Hummer. I didn't want to move on from a comfortable spot.

Anyway, fourth grade, I got out of Catholic school and entered a public school. It wasn't a bad area, and it wasn't a bad school, but it wasn't something that I was used to. Due to the stigma placed on public schools, the public school was perceived as a downward move.

As society labels things again, it was almost considered the ghetto. Everyone knows how this is, when a kid comes from a certain school, or they are moving down from private schools, then it is perceived as "Oh, you're from the ghetto school" or "Oh, you're going to the ghetto school."

It doesn't matter if it was right or wrong, but it's just how it was. Making the move to the public-school system, I met a lot of different people. It's not that kids in a public school are bad kids, or that the kids in a private school are better; you just go in there, and you meet whoever you meet.

It didn't help that I had two external perspectives on fighting. Mom always wanted me to just fall to the ground and act like I got hurt when I was in a fight. Dad always wanted me to stick up for myself. I remember distinctively; he used to say, "that you have an imaginary line between yourself and them, and if someone crosses your imaginary line, go ahead and smack them."

With these two confusing and conflicting parental perspectives concerning my fighting, I continued my immature mentality. I could go to mom after having a fight. My Mom would say, "I told you to fall down." She would fall into motherly love and cuddle me. My dad couldn't really say anything because he was proud that I whipped this kid's ass, but yet I was still in trouble. My dad would tell me not to fight if I could avoid it. My brothers saw that I could get away with almost anything with my parents, which I am sure frustrated them, and the idea always stuck with me. This mentality only continued to grow.

It was a big part of my own internal conflict. Did it negatively reinforce the behavior? Of course, it did. It was giving me mixed feelings. Dad wanted me to do what he thought was right, which was to stick up for myself. And then, of course, I had to tell him why I did it. Not that any of the fights were justifiable. I'm not condoning anyone of the fights. Though an example of what my father saw as "okay" was when a kid stole my bicycle at school and then rode it the next day. I got into school, saw it, and went to take back my bike. My anger escalated when the kid said: "Oh, this is my brother's bike." Of course, then we were rolling on the ground.

I got my bike back, but a fight is a fight. At school, the rule was: if you get into a fight, you get suspended. I'd see and understand that fighting wasn't proper, but I didn't care. I was starting to build such a big reputation at school that the idea encouraged me to fight. It turned into a beast that was growing inside of me. There was this constant "what-did-you-say-about-me? What-did-you-say-about-mom? What-did-you-say-about-my-brothers?" mentality because I found that it was the only way I could get respect.

Despite my growing reputation as a short-tempered fighter, I had no idea what people actually thought of me because nobody would talk to me. I even had a fight with a girl. During sixth grade, this game called "Letter B" became really popular. The rules were if you said any word starting with B, they would punch you until you said, "Okay, letter B." This girl was sitting next to me one day when we had a substitute teacher. We swore into the game with our pinky fingers crossed. But after a while, I was getting to the point where I actually wanted to do some work for the first time in school. I ended up saying a word that started with B, and she started hitting me in the arm, and I said, "Hey, I don't want to play anymore." Then she said, "You said the letter B." I said, "No, bitch. I'm not playing anymore." So that was another B word, so she kept hitting me, and that was it.

I stood up, the desks cleared, and everybody moved out of the way. She came at me with claws. She cut my face with her nails, so I hit her in the face about five times. I won the battle but went down to the office after the incident. I had a bad feeling in my gut about fighting with a female. That's an unspoken rule, never hit a girl.

That brings me back to what I was saying in the introduction. What is life? You're always looking back through things that now could be questioned—was it right? Was it wrong? Did I do the right thing? Did I not do the right thing? There are so many complicated times like that during childhood because we really don't have a true understanding of what the hell we're doing. You're getting mixed feelings, vibrations, and understandings of whether you're doing the right or wrong thing. At the end of the day, it doesn't really matter, but there's the truth part of it.

I know that it was tough for my parents because at one point I had a lot of anger that came out. I told them I wanted to go live with my grandparents in Massachusetts. I knew this hurt, my parents. I was just pent up with all these ideas, and it's just something that I blamed my parents for. I felt that I was right. My frustrated ideas caused me to lose my parent's trust.

I would then have to fight to earn that trust back. How could you go and get expelled from middle school and your parents still believe everything you say, right? Through my spoiled nature, I would manipulate my way back into mom's arms. It was the same routine of fight and cry. It just was a terrible circle. My brothers saw this and chose a different path.

There was a lot of animosity between my brothers and I growing up, based on my behavior. They thought "How can you stick up for this little bastard when he's getting into fights all the time? You're always yelling at me if I'm getting in trouble, but you're never doing a damn thing to him." My dad and mom never really hit us, but we got our spankings. At times, my dad would spank us because it was his only way of dealing with everything. I remember that, and now that I'm raising three kids, I don't spank them. I fear I'm instilling the idea of what persists from your childhood, must be how life is. It's the idea of what you resist, that persists.

Being spanked by my father, who was frustrated with me, was part of my childhood. It was his idea of life that was instilled in me: the kid isn't doing what you want them to do. Therefore you're upset, and the only way that I could get you to listen is when I whip your ass. The way I treat my daughters today has a lot to do with negative connotations that came from my father disciplining me. It would lead me down the road that gave me trouble later on in life.

I experienced the belief that it was okay to hit others when I was frustrated. It shaped me into a particular person. I was so young at the time that it turned into my belief system. A system that was so strong the only way I could get out was through a complete breakdown. Only then was I able to start to see the truth and question everything that had festered in my youth.

It was all based on the spoiled and egotistical mindset I had developed. It was a mixture of fear and my need to control every part of my life. I discovered later in life: the more your childhood contains fear and control-type behaviors, the more likely you will repeat this behavior in your adult life if you don't start to question ingrained beliefs.

Now, let me state this: there were times when I had a lot of great things happen, too. I don't ever want to solely focus on the negatives. There are a lot of great memories that I have of us playing baseball. My dad had a batting cage in the backyard, and he'd flip baseballs to us. My brothers and I would play pee wee baseball or T-ball, and we made the all-star teams. We had a lot of "glory days," as they say.

We had a lot of wonderful times, and at one point I even got a Go Kart for Christmas, the spoiled brat that I was. My brothers were like, "How the hell does this kid pull this off every year?" What I know today is that a materialistic environment makes you become what you are. We put a label on it that says, "you have to have this." When you do, you can say "Now I'm happy." And I think that's the ego. That's the search for happiness. That's the part that would drive you to the edge because you'll never satisfy of it. You'll never find it all. You're spending all your time seeking it, and it drives you to the point where you don't want to live anymore.

I felt this way because I was so frustrated, that I couldn't get mad at anybody anymore. If someone would drive me up the wall, it didn't make it right for me to try to fight them. Since being a child, I had a paradigm in my mind that the only way I could solve issues was through a fight or the only way to win a war was to go to war. My attitude was "Hey, you know what, I'm going to get what I want, and piss-on-you." That was bigotry.

It's all a fear-based mentality, the fear of the unknown. Instead, you should just live life and stop trying to prove yourself all the time. Stop trying to be the projected definition of what somebody else says. If you want to be an artist, be an artist. If you want to achieve something in life, then do it. However, don't be something simply because that's what you've been told you have to do or what you believe that you have to do.

As a kid, no one understands this; especially when you're spoiled. Instead, you see things in a black and white manner according to what you grew up with, your ingrained beliefs. For me, it was that way. I was caught up in believing things that didn't make any sense.

Fighting Will

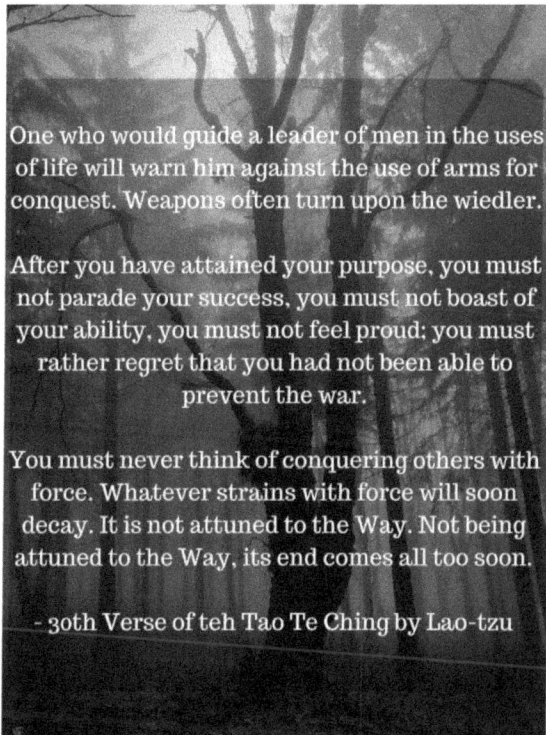

One who would guide a leader of men in the uses of life will warn him against the use of arms for conquest. Weapons often turn upon the wiedler.

After you have attained your purpose, you must not parade your success, you must not boast of your ability, you must not feel proud; you must rather regret that you had not been able to prevent the war.

You must never think of conquering others with force. Whatever strains with force will soon decay. It is not attuned to the Way. Not being attuned to the Way, its end comes all too soon.

- 30th Verse of teh Tao Te Ching by Lao-tzu

CHAPTER 3: HIGH SCHOOL

Being around the pro-athletes from a young age, it influenced me to want to become one. I had my first paying job when I was seven years old as a bat boy for the Boston Red Sox. I worked in the clubhouse with my older brothers. Working together and around the professional baseball players created this desire in me to be a pro-athlete; it was ingrained in me.

My desire wasn't from the promise of great fortune. Our family didn't go without, my father worked his ass off, and we had plenty to survive. I wanted to be a pro-athlete because I thought that was fame. It went hand in hand with my type-A personality and egotistical mindset: this is a kick ass guy. You hear about the Bo Jacksons of the world and how famous and popular they were. I wanted a part of that fame. A portion of the problem was not knowing the effort that it took for Bo Jackson to become a pro. I thought it was just a case of playing, and that I'd then simply get fame with no consideration of the sacrifices it would take to get it. Oh, what a spoiled mind!

That thirst for fame increased when I started to make the all-star team when playing baseball. I started to think "Oh, man, I'm making all-stars every year. I must have a shot." I played baseball all the way through my eighth-grade year. Then I played American Legion, which was the varsity level for the high school. But when I went to high school, the coach made everybody try out. I got cut from the program because I didn't have a strong enough arm.

Now, my father has a love for baseball. He still plays fantasy baseball, and he's got a big collection of sports memorabilia. Baseball was probably the biggest impact in my life growing up, so I was driven to baseball in search of my fame. After the try-outs in high school, my father approached the head coach and said, "Why did you cut him? Why didn't you put him on JV?" And the coach basically said, "There's no room, I don't have a spot for him. He needs to get his arms stronger." Then the question became how do you get stronger arms if you're not playing?

Playing sports in high school started to level me out a little bit from the fighting and the anger I felt. My father said, "go play football," once I got cut from the baseball team. So, I tried out for football. When I got to play, I learned pretty quickly it's not easy being 5'9 and 189lbs going up against a senior that's around 280lbs. They used to call me the Little Chihuahua on the field because I would fight and not give in despite my size. You'd have to kill me to get me off of them. Even the 275lbs guys would push me around a little bit more, but I'd still be kicking ass and making them work.

Playing sports in high school got me away from that paradigm that I was stuck in. It showed me that there was something more to my life as I always had that gut-wrenching feeling; intuition that people talk about, a deep feeling in your heart, after a fight. I never really wanted to hurt people deliberately, so I never felt good after a fight. But it felt good to be macho. For example, once in eighth grade, there was a student that was fighting the PE teacher. I stood in front of the kid, and I started beating the hell out of him for hitting a teacher, and I got expelled because it was my last straw.

My father had to go to a hearing. He was a school teacher at the time, so he knew the superintendents and everyone else. He had to represent me as my attorney. He was able to get me back into school to finish because otherwise I would have been held back.

Don't take that lightly. I got expelled. I was out of school a week, but I was suspended so many times, whether it was from being insubordinate or from fighting. I'd piss a teacher off, and I had to serve detention. So, once you get three weeks of suspensions, the next time they'd say, "Hey, you got to get the hell out of here."

I had to see a psychiatrist a couple of times at a young age. This was to try and figure out why I was so angry, why I wasn't acting like the other kids. The issue stemmed from having no self-reliance. I wasn't allowed to do what I truly wanted all the time, but I was still just a kid. I don't think anybody wants to be locked into anything; whether a job or relationship. There is a statistic that says 87% of all people working in the USA do not like their jobs [Washington post By Jena McGregor October 10, 2013] and have a higher percentage of heart attacks on Mondays. Today, I can speak about what was behind all of that, but back then, I didn't know any of that.

I was driven from what they thought I should be; 'they' could refer to parents or teachers. They evaluated me on several occasions. Once was based around the intellectual side of things to see if I was capable, or if I really did have a learning disability.

Later on, because we didn't live in any particular school district, my father, knew that he could get me into a new high school, but I had to go to a psychiatrist first. The psychiatrist had to write a letter stating that I had all these troubles in life and needed a new start. So, I got into a new high school.

Winter Haven is where my parents lived and where I grew up. That was where the school in my eighth-grade year that I was expelled from was located. A lot the kids that I had fights with had trouble with went to Winter Haven. My parents thought that it would be a good idea to send me to a new school, and it was. They were building a brand-new school that was a little outside my current district. Dad drove me every morning until I was old enough to ride with friends who drove. It was the best thing that could have happened at that point in my life. At that point, it must be remembered that I was still a young kid. I didn't really know what the was going on.
There was a lot of misunderstanding with me growing up. I did not understand anything about what I was doing or

why I was doing it. I can tell you that my oldest brother and I had a bad fight when I was about 10 or 11. He hit me in the head and my nose poured with blood. I walked down the hallway, bleeding. Mom was pissed off because blood was all over the floor.

However, one of the biggest fights that I think I had with my oldest brother happened in high school. I was probably a freshman at the time. He was at home and had to pick up mom from work. However, before he went to do that we fought. We were home alone as both my dad and mom were working. We had this fight, and I lost because he was older. Then he ran to the car and hauled ass to go and fetch mom. So, there I was, grabbing a bat because I was so far into my ways at that point. I may have been a freshman coming out of that system, but either way, I was at a spot in my life where I was a very angry kid. It was my brother John who came out and said, "Don't ruin our name. Don't come out of the house with this stupid ass bat." I was going to hit the car and hit him with it.

It made me think, "What do you mean 'ruin the name?' What the hell does that mean?" So, I received all these mixed messages, and at the time it was very confusing because I didn't know what was meant by 'our name?' There were a lot of these experiences that became part of this driven psyche, but they all came to a crash later on in my life.

I've always had a strong sense of soul within me that even when having a fight with my brother. It didn't feel right, even though I felt good during it. So, I was told I'd be going to a new school at Lake Region. I was given a new opportunity. I was given an outlet to get away from people that were a bad influence on me. Moving me to this school is where my parents did a great job in my upbringing.

That new school beginning was also the start of a new drive in me. My parents told me that it would be great: "It's going to be a new beginning. You're not going to be around the same crew." Even in middle school, I got tied up with the skipping squads who would sneak out drinking beer at 13 or 14 years old. Whether you define it as 'immoral,' I think those kids still have a soul in them, because everybody does. Either way, my parents, and brothers were relieved because I was out of that situation and away from some friends who pulled me into bad habits. They knew I was at a new school and soon would be driving.

Even at the new high school, I got into some trouble, because I was still coming out of those old habits and beliefs which were hard to break initially. It wasn't like I was looking for fights though because I saw mature kids and I realized that there were attractive girls around me. I thought, "Oh cool, there are the physiques that I saw in some magazines that my brothers showed me." So, all of a sudden I was faced with this, rather than the previous immaturity I had known. But it wasn't possible to just walk up to a senior and ask her out. She wouldn't have wanted to go out with a freshman. You kind of see this different perspective now and begin to see how life flows in high school. The teachers are different, too; in high school, they're not so driven by discipline. They recognize that students are growing into adulthood, and are learning to be responsible for themselves.

It was at this point, in a new public high school, that I had an epiphany. I didn't really want to fight anymore; although I would when I needed to. Thankfully, I was coming out of that adolescent mindset. I was going through puberty and growing into a man, rather than behaving like a boy. It was rewarding, too. I was starting to see my body change from a chubby build to more muscular frame, and I wasn't picked on as much.

My parents saw this change too, and that's why my father said, "You know what, just go out for football." As I stated earlier. The football coach that happened to be there was pretty well-known in the public eye. This is where my dad being a sports fanatic really came into play. My dad knows it all. You could ask him anything history-wise about sports, and he knows it. One of the things that my dad understood at the time was that the football coach at the high school was an impressive one. He was a head coach at one point and won the Florida Gators' first-ever top-ten finish.

His name was Charley Pell and he was just a wonderful human being, too. He had a warm heart and a love for the game. It was a cool experience. Going out for football as a freshman at a new school, I lettered. We were playing before 10,000 to 11,000 fans there. You know as a freshman, I didn't actually get to play, but I was on the sidelines thinking, "whoa, this is definitely a big change."

Since I was finally getting into other sports besides baseball, I started seeing other things happening around me. I was being involved in really cool things and finally felt a change in me; it helped to calm the anger issues for me. High school sports were a great environment, and it changed my ego. Whether it was for better or worse, it changed it. It changed it in a way that was driven by a pro-athlete mentality.

The fame focus was starting to come out again because I got to go to a pep rally and the entire school was there. The procedure was that they called you out, and then they would clap and scream; just for you. What's funny is that they didn't even know who the hell I was. But because I was part of the varsity football team, they clapped and screamed. That started to quickly build a different part of ego for me. It was a realization that, "Oh, wait a minute, I don't have to fight to get what I want. Now I'm doing something that people like me for."

I started to get recognized more and more, and it's almost like that popularity belt: once you become more popular, people see you in the lunch room, and they don't ignore you anymore. People believe that you must be tough because you play football, and you work out all the time, and other kids notice this. Then you start to develop into a different role.

I was still questioning life, just like I am questioning it today. However, at the same time, it's all part of life. It's part of growing and pushing through those issues. It is about having to go through decisions you've made. I wasn't born at 36. I was born and had to go and experience these things. I lettered, I grew even more, because not a lot of people lettered during their freshman year.
I knew things were changing; I just didn't realize how much. For example, because I wasn't getting detention or being in trouble all the time, I felt I was coming out of that

funk. Of course, I still had a little bit of that paradigm in me, and I smarted off to one of the teachers. The athletic director was in there, so he told me to come in on a Saturday.

Saturday rolled around, and I headed up there. I remember that I was in a golf cart and the athletic director said, "You know, there's something about you that makes me feel compelled to say that I don't think you're so damn tough, and that you really don't want to be out here." Of course, my smart-ass A-personality said, "Hey, you don't want to be out here, either, you know." What kind of stupid-ass question is that? Of course, I don't want to be out here, but I'm out here. So, he got frustrated with me for the comment, but he stuck it out, and he said, "You know what, let's see how tough you are. Go play a sport that's tougher, like wrestling." My response was something like, "Yeah, whatever. What's wrestling got to do with being tough? I'm fine."

But he put the seed in my head. It was part of the transformation of coming out of that kick ass mentality, all that "I-can-kick-everybody's-ass mentality" to "Okay-fine-I'll-go." It was a challenge at that point. I've always had this in me. Never tell me I can't do a certain thing. Sports or anything, if you challenge me, I will accept it to prove you wrong.

When I was little, I was skilled with building things. I've always had an engineering and artistic mind. When I was about six or seven, I went home one day and saw the phone hanging on the wall. For some reason, I took it down and took it apart. And after I took it apart, my dad was furious. He yelled, "We're going to have to buy another phone." And my mom kind of talked him out and said, "No, watch what he does." After I had taken apart the phone, I rebuilt it and made a phone call. It was working fine. I could do this with anything.

I always looked for a way to get involved, and I think that that was also a big part of high school. When the director challenged me, I still had a little bit of that attitude in me. I was like "Wait a minute, you're telling me I can't wrestle, man? I could kick all of these guys' asses, you know." So, I went out and tried wrestling. I didn't do it right away, but the wrestling coach was also the earth-science teacher at that time. He was really cool with me, and there I was, coming from football. I had a big chip on my shoulder that was like, "Yeah, I'm the star football player as a freshman."

I got to work out with the weightlifting coach, which is when I really started finding my niche. The coach was really trying to drive the school to have a weightlifting team. He had a team at his previous school. And when he developed it, he was considered one of the best weightlifting coaches in town. He really took a liking to me because he saw that I never stopped, I always gave my all. He was also on the coaching staff for our football team. Anytime there was, "Hey, I need a volunteer," I was always the guy that jumped out and said, "Hey, I want to be in that spot." I've always busted my ass. I always had that will power.

The wrestling coach saw the work ethic I had and said, "Just give me three days to work with you in wrestling." Every day when I was in class, he would always chirp this to me. It was becoming a constant nagging. So, I called him out and said, "Man what makes you think you're so tough?" Because this guy was 145lbs and about 35 or so.

The wrestling coach turned out to be a great coach. He won a national championship at his college, little did I know. I thought I'd still kick his ass, but he was like, "Come out, give me three days," but I said, "Fine, that's all you want? Three days?" He said, "Yeah, but if you quit before the three days, I'll have the right to call you a pussy." I was blown away that he was calling me out. He didn't do this in front of everybody. He called me aside instead of saying this in front of the whole class.

I went to practice that very same day. I said to the weightlifting coach that I wanted three days to go to the wrestling team. The weightlifting coach responded, "don't come back then." So that was a huge blow to me. There I was, trying to figure out life and he told me that? My reaction was 'what the heck? Who the hell does this guy think he is? I'll wrestle, and I'll lift weights. He doesn't tell me what I can and can't do.' So, I said, "fine, forget it."

At that point, I was all fired up and completely committed to wrestling. I went out for wrestling and went in there and picked up one of the teammembers because I used to watch WWF. My brothers and I used to wrestle on the floor. So, I wrestled like that, by picking a guy up and slamming him down on the ground. I'm 185lbs, and I'm wrestling a guy that might have been 160. They said, "Hey, you can't wrestle like that. There are actually rules to wrestling." That surprised me.
I think that helped with my aggression. I had to learn the techniques otherwise I wouldn't have been able to compete. The discipline was adding to the transformation

into what I became. I stayed on the team. I didn't quit. I was on junior varsity for most of the year. Towards the end of the year, I started getting pretty good, and I even lost some weight. There was a guy on the team who was a senior, and I pinned him. What surprised me is that this senior had wrestled hard that whole year and he was getting ready to go to districts.

Even with that boost of confidence, the spoiled brat came out of me again to smother the positive feeling. At first, I thought, "Shit, I beat him. I should wrestle." Instead, I got the idea "No, how can I ever beat a senior—the guy who kicked everyone's butt—all year long? All because I pinned him one time?" I probably would have been a good wrestler, but instead of staying, I became spoiled again and said, "Piss on you, I'm not going to wrestle anymore, then." So, I did that one year, and that was it. I basically let my ego take over because of that one experience, and I threw away that opportunity. It left me with only football.

When things are going well for me, I excel. If there's something that I want to do, I'm all in. I was like a leech. You had to peel me off in order to get me to stop doing something. It was a part of the fighting and growing up, and battling for this trophy that was never even a trophy.

At this point, I was a sophomore. Charley Pell stepped out of the football coaching position because it was just too stressful for him and his wife, so my sophomore year wasn't as fulfilling. At this point, I was back on junior varsity after lettering as a freshman. That ego of mine kicked in as it did for the wrestling, and I said, "I don't want to play football anymore because I'm not on varsity.

This sucks." Even though it was the coach's decision that I needed to develop more, I believed that I had developed enough to make it on varsity for my freshman year. All of a sudden, I found myself back on junior varsity. That was a hard thing for me to cope with since I had given football my all.

The vicious cycle hit me again. So, I said, "You know what? I'll just transfer then because this sucks and I want to play." I ended up leaving the school that started me in a good direction. I transferred back to the high school that had a lot of my old friends again.

I entered Winter Haven as a junior and started back where all my other friends were. I had an opportunity to play on a team that was going to play me every day there. I was the new guy in the field, and everyone had to pause and think "wait a minute, he's strong." I had a technique that a lot of guys didn't, and I was always strong.

My oldest brother already had experience in lifting weights, and I was always trying to lift stuff. I always had strength even when I was little. I remember a time when I tried to pick up an old antique iron that my papa had in his basement at the age of two or three. Or on other occasions when my grandparents would visit, and I'd go to the rental car and grab all their suitcases out of the back. I was around four or five years old trying to pick up a damn suitcase that weighed more than me. I have always had a strong back. The competition was fun because at that point I was a junior. I had developed a strong body, and I was working out hard. That was a good transfer as I was the new dog in the pack and nobody knew what I was capable of. So, they kind of just let me roam, and when they introduced me at the beginning of games, it felt good. It wasn't like I didn't have the experience. They saw me as a veteran who knew what he was doing. They knew I'd come from Lake Region and had experience. I made varsity in my junior and senior year.

When I started out in the public school, I had a hard time building friendships and trying to find my own identity. Making friends never really worked out. However, this time I knew all people who were there. They knew me. So, it was easy to build into my own clique.

Then I met Germaine and Brian. They turned into some of the best friends that I ever had. However, I was a year behind them. They graduated, and it left me feeling adrift because I didn't go out with others often. The high school mentality was that alcohol and partying was what it took to be cool. I never really got into that after a horrible experience smoking weed when I was a junior.

Growing up, I developed a fear of horror movies. My older brothers and I would watch scary horror movies way back when I was really little and it kept me in my mom's bed a few nights. Freddy Krueger and Jason that were the worst for me! Once during my junior year, I was smoking weed and it had to be a bad batch of it. It was laced with something. Here we are, sneaking out of the house. My buddy's car was stuck a bit and we were trying to push it out of the grass. We didn't want to wake anybody up, and here I was stoned. I'm looking down the street, not caring what hour it is, and hallucinating that Freddy Krueger is out there in the middle of the street.

One day, I was stoned with my brother, and we were at a friend's house. The movie *Natural Born Killers* begins in black and white and the screen is turning. Since I had already experienced a problem with some bad weed a few weeks previously, I thought I was hallucinating again. I told my brother, "You got to take me home." I wigged out, but I got home.

That was a breakthrough moment in my life. I freaked out so much that I was lying on the couch and my mom asked if we had been smoking. I said, "yeah, we were smoking cigarettes." But marijuana has a strong, distinctive smell. I'm sure she knew I was lying. I was still spinning in my head about what I had seen in the movie.

My mom was a very understanding mother. I could go to her for anything. When I said anything related to sex-ed, or anything at all, she never would laugh or judge. She was my psychologist. She was perfect for that kind of stuff.

She knew something was up and I started crying. She knew exactly what was going on. I was tripping out a little bit, so she calmed me. She didn't make much of it because she knew what to do. The next morning, she let me know what she wanted to say. She was even very kind at that point, just the nurturing mother that I needed because I had a breakdown, thinking "what am I doing?"

I was starting to see everything they worked so hard to do—the morals, all the good and bad. You know, don't do this, don't do that. I was starting to see myself going down a path that I wouldn't want to necessarily project. Some people end up having addictions, and I became fearful of that. So, I cried, and I swore that I would not do that ever again. I got so wrapped around their fingers that I woke up saying, "I want to go to church."

I ended up spending a lot of time going to the movies and hanging out with my parents. It was kind of lonely since my two good friends were off in college.

I had finally regained my parent's trust at this point. I was going to church every Sunday and was just doing things that I felt good about. So, on the weekends, my mom and dad would lend me the car, and I'd go drive over to the University of South Florida because my friends were attending college there. At that point, I started to see how they were acting. I was actually becoming more mature to the point that when I would see the way my high school peers were acting, I thought they were so immature. It was a weird feeling looking down at them saying, "This is kind of lame. You guys are just kids. You'll figure it out," as though I was the adult. Like I knew everything; of course, I didn't. It was just because I was hanging out with college kids.

Don't get me wrong; I still had some childhood tendencies. I went and got a fake ID so that we could go to clubs. I was 18, and I was legally able to get in, but I would still go drinking a couple of times here and there. Because I was around my friends, I felt more comfortable doing it.

So, there I was, this big macho football player in my senior year. I didn't even go to my senior prom because I thought it was lame. I was nominated for the homecoming court, but I didn't really care. I felt that it was below me. Hanging out with my college friends, I thought I was more mature than other students my age.

The biggest lesson that I learned from all of these experiences was: Don't be in a hurry to grow up. I think that there's a natural progression that takes place. Just let it naturally exist and come to you. I'm saying that you need to let this "you" come out on its own. There's something that takes place that gives you a little fear, a little courage, and a little more self-reliance.

Try to find yourself because now you have the intellect to do so. During the younger years, you don't really have that. Just enjoy being young, but still, find yourself. If you're battling through that, try not to take everything so serious.

Just enjoy it because it goes by pretty fast. I've found that some people have experiences during high school they hated. I actually enjoyed high school because it got me out of my funk. I had a totally different experience than some others.

It's important not to allow the external influences of other people to define who you are. Let the internal perspective be your drive towards discovering your true identity. That's the power of will that we all have. We all have that choice. When we don't follow that choice of will, then life sucks. Life becomes tough because of the definitions from other people. When we start to make our own definitions, we grow beyond what we have learned and start making up our own minds about life.

The ancient masters were profound and subtle. Their wisdom was unfathomable. There is no way to describe it. One can only describe them vaguely by thier appearance.

Watchful, like men crossing a winter stream. Alert, like men aware of danger. Simple as uncarved wood. Hollow like caves. Yielding, like ice about to melt. Amporhous, like muddy water.

But the muddiest water clears as it is stilled. And out of that stillness life arises.

He who keeps the Tao does not want to be full. But precisely because he is never full, he can remain like a hidden sprout and does not rush to early ripening.

- 15th Verse of the Tao Te Ching by Lao-tzu

CHAPTER 4: AFTER HIGH SCHOOL

One thing that happened when I played high school football was that I suffered from a lot of physical pain. My routine became: I'd play, practice and see a chiropractor. Senior year my neck was bad, so I would go see a chiropractor, and they'd crack my neck, and I'd go back home. It was crazy. There was a revolving door, and I would see them almost every day before practice. At one point in my senior year, I was crying to my parents. I looked them in the eyes with tears running down my face, "I don't want to play anymore because my damn arm is numb and I can't feel my fingers." All kinds of injuries were going on in my arms and back. I was tired of all of it. I'd start to feel good; then I started to get stingers. It felt like a burning sensation down my arm until I got a little sigh of relief from the chiropractic adjustment.

After having the pain, I wasn't sure that I wanted to play football when I went to college. I also started to wonder if

I should even apply when I barely graduated high school. I didn't excel; I didn't push myself academically because of my stubbornness. I even had to take the high school comprehensive test a couple of times to graduate. That was a struggle, and I started losing a little bit of my confidence. Eventually, I passed the test, and I graduated. I got a diploma. Because of that experience, I found myself thinking that there's no way I could attend college. That hurt and I started doubting my skills and my ability.

I also didn't know if I could handle going up against a grown man in college because you might be hitting against somebody that's 20 or 22 years old. You're hitting somebody that's been there a while. My father would go to a college, and he would bring home a book that showed what some of the football players looked like. He was trying to encourage me to go because he'd say, "Oh, look at this guy. He signed on and looked at his stats." Then I'd read about him. He wasn't much bigger than me, and he wasn't that much stronger.

It gave me some confidence to start looking at some small schools. One of them, Concordia, came down to see me play football. It was an uplifting experience. Coaches that wanted me to play on their team up in Wisconsin came down to see me. Finally, it was Murray State that I ended up choosing the college I wanted to attend.

My dad took me all the way up to Kentucky to attend Murray State. My father graduated from there, so that was a big influence on me, to decide to go to that college. It was a larger school than what I was used to. Colleges are divided into divisions I, II and III. The divisions are formed with regard to their athletics and are directly correlated to their ability to offer athletic scholarships. Murray wasn't a division I-AA. It was like USF where I started.

I would have probably played a lot more at some of the better division three schools. However, I ended up taking this route in the I-AA. I was a very strong guy. Out of 110 guys on the football team at Murray State, I was number three in the area of strength for the entire team. That was a confidence builder, and I met some guys the first night that I was there that became instant friends.

One of the guys that I'll never forget was Harris. He inspired me a lot because he was playing while in remission from leukemia. He was an all-American in high school. They had him projected to be the next quarterback for Tennessee, and he's from Memphis. So, he was all in. I mean, this guy was great. When his high school found out that he was sick, he lost his scholarships. However, Murray kept his scholarships because they never found out. They thought he had mono because his lymph nodes were swollen up underneath his arms. Harris survived the Leukemia and is still in remission. He battled it, he beat it and played football once again.

And then there was a guy named Brian from Mississippi. We knew that one of the parts of training was that we had to run up the stairs in the stadium. But the stadium at Murray was seven stories straight up. I had told Brian, "I'm going to walk up to the top of this thing so I'd get used to the heights because I'm not a fan of heights. I can run all the way up, but I just don't like the way it looks." So, Brian said, "I understand that. I'll do it with you." We ended up walking all the way up. They were two of the greatest friends that I made on the team.

College was a fun time, up until the point where I got hurt. I was playing linebacker, and at practice, we had to do tackling skills, to perfect them a little bit. There was a particular player who wasn't too fond of me, and I wasn't too fond of him. He wasn't liked by a lot of guys because he was the guy that would get injured a lot but had a lot of potential. He had a bad back and went through some tough times with his own personal physical abilities. At that time, I was making a name for myself in the weight room. I don't know if he saw me as competition or he just wanted to see who was tougher. He was 245lbs, and I went full speed, and we hit. My shoulder hurt very badly. He had to take his helmet off, and I began to worry I might have given him a slight concussion. He came up to me later and said nobody has ever hit me as hard as you did before. I said, "You know what, my shoulder's done."

I did rehab for about six to eight weeks. It was my left shoulder that was injured. Now my right shoulder was getting stingers similar to in high school. The doctor thought it was an AC separation, which was a pretty common part of the clavicle bone to be injured. So, they were trying to rehab that because when they saw the X-Ray, it didn't show as broken.

Even with the therapy, I wasn't getting any better. I was getting discouraged, and my studies struggled. I was starting down that spoiled path again.

I think the coaches were really starting to see my changed attitude because the defense coordinator asked me "Are you playing football for your dad? Are you playing for yourself?" I immediately went to my vicious cycle. I was pissed. I was like, "Fuck you. I'm fourteen hundred miles away from my parents. They don't ever come see me. My shoulder hurts, I'm tired. I'm tired of this." I really got upset.

Finally, I said to my dad, "This isn't getting any better." My mom, being a nurse at that time, said, "I'll see if I can get you some samples, some anti-inflammatory samples to try to help you sleep." She sent me some stuff, but it didn't help me much. I was literally crying myself to sleep because I was lying down on my back in some of the worst pain I'd ever been in; not knowing the truth of what had really happened.

The spring game came and went. I didn't play because my body hurt so badly. Before spring break my mother and father said, "Bring home your records, and we'll go get a second opinion." So, I went home for spring break, and I saw a doctor in Winter Haven who made me hold a sandbag during the X-Ray. The sand bag was 10lbs, and it separated my clavicle. It was then that he saw that it was broken. The truth was discovered that I had gone ten weeks with a broken clavicle. When they did an MRI, they saw that I had some problems in the torn tissue, but because I had my range of motion, it was decided I had nursed it back to health. But it was extremely painful. I still had to let the bone heal up.

This experience led me to the decision that I didn't want to play football anymore. My left shoulder was hurt, my collar bone had cracked, and my neck had started to bother me so much that I was done. I quit college.

Now that I was no longer playing football or taking college classes, I started thinking about my artistic skills. In high school, it was always art classes that I excelled in. I had several art pieces that received ribbons. My mother was a huge influence on me, with regards to pursuing art, since I was done with Murray State.

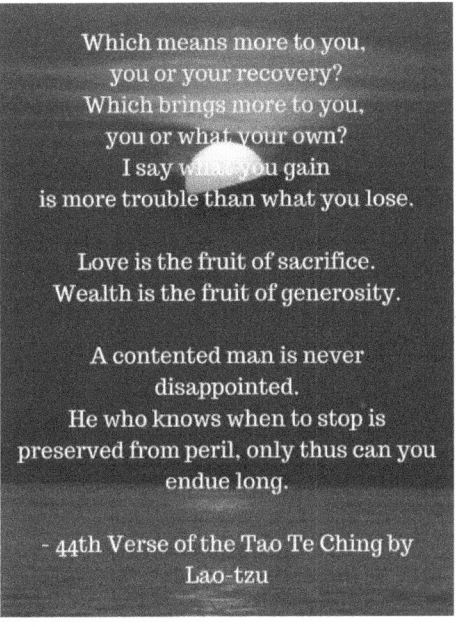

Which means more to you,
you or your recovery?
Which brings more to you,
you or what your own?
I say what you gain
is more trouble than what you lose.

Love is the fruit of sacrifice.
Wealth is the fruit of generosity.

A contented man is never disappointed.
He who knows when to stop is preserved from peril, only thus can you endue long.

- 44th Verse of the Tao Te Ching by Lao-tzu

When I was a young child, after I'd gotten my angel picture published, I started doing more and more artwork. It was a little bit of an egotistical thing too. I learned that when I drew something, I got rewarded for it. When I drew something really good, it felt nice to see my mom and dad smile. They were very appreciative, and my mom was especially fond of the art. She loved everything that I did, and she was the one who pushed me along. I'm very grateful for that.

I remember drawing a Mickey Mouse. I did it with a pen, and it turned out looking identical to Mickey. These things just kept transpiring. I just kept getting better with practice. In middle school, I started little pieces here and there. I also had my art classes. In high school, my art teacher was really encouraging, and she just loved the work that I could produce. I had several pieces that went to the local mall, and they would often win first prize; it just escalated from there.

I got better at learning techniques and shading. I really started to bring out the dimensional side of things. The medium I enjoyed most was pencil and charcoal. I didn't do a whole lot of painting, but I did charcoal drawings really well. I liked using clay as well. I didn't get into the clay until I was in the eleventh grade. I created a three-dimensional picture of a bass.

The more I got in tune with my creativity, the better I got at it. I took some classes in college, and some of my drawings really started to pop at that point. In my apartment at College, I was really into Italian stuff, like DeNiro and Pashley, so I would draw them. My buddy Keith said, "you should put those in the mall like they used to sell. I don't know if they still do or not, but they would sell these pictures." He suggested I copy them to sell. That really built my confidence up.

One of my art teachers said, "I want you to do this gesture this way." Well, it didn't fit the way I drew, so I would get annoyed or upset, but I would do it, and the picture wouldn't turn out the way I wanted it to. So, I started drawing the way I just knew how to, without any teaching. That's my answer towards questioning the truth. I ended up doing better my own way versus someone else's way. Once at college, my teacher said to me, "you're drawing from the inside out. You're supposed to draw from the outside in and with a gesture." I said, "look, I tried it your way. I don't like to do it that way. If it doesn't turn out exactly the way it looks from this still life picture, I'll go back to your way." Well, when it was time to critique it, there was probably nothing on the paper that didn't look the same as the photo. So, she couldn't say anything at all. We were critiqued by peers, and they said, "that's freaking awesome." So, you could see almost this furious, pissed off teacher, thinking, 'this asshole didn't do it my way, but it looks really good.' She did compliment me on how well it looked. That was another rewarding feeling towards my art. It felt like I could produce good products, and people liked my work.

When I created a drawing, I had nothing more to think about than creating what I was looking at. I would attempt to put it down on paper, to capture the expression. So, even though I may have music in the background, or I may have been listening to headphones, that didn't mean that I wasn't focused on drawing. Drawing definitely is therapeutic and keeps me living in the present. When I get the feeling to draw, it's impulsive, and I need to draw right that second. When we put our full attention to the power of how strong we are, things will show up on paper. Thirty hours later, you're looking at it, and you're like, damn, I just drew a masterpiece. How the hell did I do it? I don't even know. I just did it.

My life inside, or what I term God life/source, can do anything. I would say, for example, I am going to draw a picture, and it would appear on paper. The downside, however, is that when I drew, I also would say no to homework and, sure enough, it showed.

Unfortunately, all too often society thinks that artistic people can only become starving artists. However, that's not true: and again, that's what we are talking about. This book is about what the truth is, right? So here I was, skeptical to do art because I was supposed to be this macho man that kicks everybody's ass. I was just full of ego. I started to fear and over think my artistic ability because I believed what society says. This silly stuff was part of my thought process all along.

Being an artist, however, can be tough. You must do installations, and you have to do this and that in order to make money as an artist. It's almost like this reality drove me not to seek any art. I heard it so many times in high school. That art was not a way to go because you're not going to make any money. Then you go off to college, and you're like, yeah, it's very difficult to make any money because you must sell your pieces. One artist told me once you sell your piece for a hundred bucks you're considered a hundred-dollar artist now. So, I was like, I'm not going to pursue art but that's where my mind was.

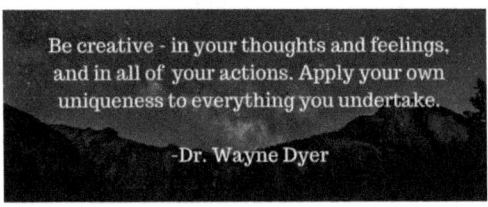

I was living at home and just trying to figure things out. One day I went up to my mom's office where she was working. I was still lifting weights. I still had this burning desire to work out because of who it made me. So, my mom said, "Why don't you just do personal training?" I was like, "That's a thought. What does that entail? What the hell is a personal trainer?" She's explained, "You know, you're physically fit, you like working out, you're at the gym, anyway. You see people in there. You can help people with what you do." That was intriguing, and I said, "I might be into this, but I need some help." I told her "I'm not a nurse. I don't know anatomy. Would you help me along?" She said, "I'll teach you what you need to know. You're a smart guy; you'll figure it out." So, I said, "What do I do?" And she said, "We'll look it up."

We started going that route. However, my dad kept telling me, "Why don't you go back to Murray? Why don't you go play football again?" I said, "Dad, I don't have any eligibility left."

I studied how to be a personal trainer. I then took the tests and did the practical. It was a great feeling passing those tests and becoming a trainer. I started working at the local gyms in Tampa. As I was doing that, my dad was still on at me about going back to school. I said, "You know what, the only thing I might consider would be graphic art."

I decided to go and study graphic art at a non-traditional school called International Academy and Design. It was an art school that was not traditionally accredited. But I was enjoying that, believe it or not. I had an interesting, and inspiring teacher; his name was Mr. Patterson. He was really cool. He didn't teach from many textbooks. He just talked, and he would talk from experiences. He didn't even have any background in graphic design until later in life. He was originally a history teacher. He opened my mind to know that we could always do other things. So, he said, "You have got to have a margin of difference in your life." I was like, "What does that mean?"

He explained that it's what separates you from everybody else. When he was a history teacher, he wanted to become a graphic artist and go and work for this big company. Years back, when people came out of the war after World War II, there was an influx of people without jobs, and they didn't know how to obtain one. Recruiters wrote letters to the public, teaching them how to get a job even when they didn't have any experience. For example, if someone was an army tank driver what they are supposed to do when they apply for a job? "Here's my resume. I know how to blow stuff up, but I don't know anything else." These recruiters found very creative ways to get people jobs. The recruiter's advice was that if a job seeker went into a company, with a letter and a resume on the back end of it, which said, "Hey, I'm not interested in a job. I just wanted to tell you about myself and get to know your company better." They would go in and meet all the people on their way before they presented this. They'd meet the secretary at the front desk, and maybe someone working in the mailroom doing their daily rounds, and then they could gather more useful information about the company. They'd write it down, they'd walk it in, put it in one of the manila envelopes, and they'd give it to the boss. So now the boss has got that on file, and he's going to read that and say, "Wow, he's not interested in a job. He just wants to introduce himself to me. What a cool way. He's taking part in my company here, and he's interested." It made people intrigued, and that's what people did when they came back from the war.

That's what Mr. Patterson learned, and that's how he landed a job at a big company, even though he was a high school history teacher. He had no background, but he used that method. He then started making more money than he ever dreamt of. That story inspired me to want to get into art even more. At that stage in my life, I thought that I should perhaps try art because I was working as a personal trainer, not really making any money. I was still living at home.

To get my life back on track, I went into the International Academy in Design and studied for many hours. I eventually transferred to the University of South Florida because I was broke. I still lived with mom and dad. I had some interest in going to college, and student loans gave me a little freedom because I had extra money. I went back to school. I took out student loans, and my buddies were still at USF. I was still lost; still didn't know what the hell I was doing. But I said, "You know what, I'm going back to school."

I started to work hard at the graphic design degree. As I progressed with the degree, I began to sabotage the idea by allowing negative thoughts to enter my mind about the future.

I started taking more art classes. At that point, I could have graduated with anything. I had so many credit hours, but I had to stay focused. It only frustrated me again. I was like, "Man, I got all these damn hours. I don't have anything to really show for it. I could graduate, but I'm not graduating. What the hell." I really didn't knuckle down as

I should have. I learned a lot in the art courses that I was taking, and I thought that's what I would graduate with a degree in graphic design.

Again, I became discouraged and didn't graduate. I was doing ok with it, up until my second semester where I started to see that I needed to thoroughly know English. This scared me. I was making flyers, then I got bored with them, because I thought, "Oh, I'm just placing this text here and this text here." My creativity felt squashed even though I was getting compliments for what I was making. It still didn't feel like it was right, and as a result, I didn't push through.

I became fearful because of the mentality of these paradigms that we get stuck in, that I'm talking about throughout this entire book. I had the fearful thought that I was going to be behind a computer, making flyers all day long. That's all I could think about. The fact that I was so creative in my artistic drawings, but I wasn't able to do that on a computer. It made me say "to hell with this." All of that was due to my insecurity.

Whenever I came up against a roadblock, I decided just to quit. I crumbled. It always came back to being spoiled, thinking that if I didn't get my way I wasn't going to do it anymore. I was still maturing through all this, but what's interesting is that I could do anything I wanted to do. If you ask me to do it, even today, if you say, "Luke, can you do it?" I'd damn sure try anything. It's interesting how all that comes out as I was developing.

At the time I was also taking language classes because it interested me since my heritage is Italian. I wanted to know the language my ancestor spoke. I was very passionate about living an Italian lifestyle, and I thought that was the only way to live. I know this was narrow-mindedness, but it's the way I felt back then. One day my Italian teacher says to me "You need to go to Italy. You have got to experience Italy." I retorted, "That sounds cool." Now at this stage in my life, I started to get a little excited again. Graphic design didn't pan out for me, but now I have a new passion, direction in life!

I started to feel like I was on top of the world because I got a scholarship to go to Italy.

© Luke Chichetto

Generations honor generations endlessly.
Cultivated in the self, virtue is realized;
cultivated in the family, virtue overflows;
cultivated in the community, virtue increases;
cultivated in the state, virtue abounds.

The Tao is everywhere;
is has become everything.
To truly see it, see it as it is.
In a person, see it as a person;
in a family, see it as a family;
in a country, see it as a country;
in a world, see it as a world.

How do I know this is true?
By looking inside myself.

- 54th Verse of the Tao Te Ching by Lao-tzu

CHAPTER 5: ITALY

After learning later in life about the law of attraction, I can look back on this story and say it absolutely happens. I won the lottery, which was perfectly timed before my trip to Italy. It was my birthday, March 14th, so I played 314. I was with my buddy Keith. I sat down and told him I was going to win $500 because that was what it paid out. He said, "You're so full of shit, why do you waste your money on that?" and I said, "Dude, it's my birthday, and it only cost me a dollar. I'm going to throw it in your face. So, don't worry about it." He said, "You're not going to win." And he was right; I didn't win; that you-can't-do-it attitude started to come out again. When I really wanted something, I would do it, but if I got discouraged, I was like, "eh, if you crack me, I was done."

But this one time I decided, "You know what? I'm going to go and win $500. You think that's not going to happen? I'm going to do it." So, I went home, and I printed out six years-worth of winning numbers. There are a thousand possibilities, and I was playing 314, so I said, "Let me go back in the years and see where the last 314 came in and see if I can hit it." I went with a pencil and scratched off every number until I found 314. 37 days later, I won $500! When you put your attention on something, it becomes your truth.

I'm a great believer in numerology; the number three has been significant to me. I had three diamonds when I got married and never knew that I was going to have three kids. I'm born in March, the third month; the number three is all around me. Denise is 9-20. 9/29 was her birthday, so the 9 month, which is divisible by three.

It was 2001 when I was getting ready for my trip to Italy, and met Denise. One night, I had a couple of friends call and say they were coming over to get me to go to a local Tampa night parade called Gasparilla. It is much smaller, but similar to Mardi Gras. However, Tampa's parade focuses on a pretend pirate invasion. I said, "The hell, you are. I got to wake up in the morning. You're not going to come get me. I'm not going to Gasparilla." If you've ever been in a really busy parade, you know what it's like. Tons of people and most of them are drinking or already drunk. There is a lot of chaos, and I wasn't a huge drinker. I would occasionally go out and have a few beers, but this time I said, "No, I don't really want to go." He said, "Well, I'm coming to get you."

He knocked on my door, and it was already 10:30pm, and I was in my boxers getting ready for bed. He sat on my couch and said, "I'm not leaving until you get dressed. Let's go." I eventually gave in and went out with them. We ended up at this guy Jim's house, which they were renting. Denise was there. She was dressed conservatively. She wasn't dressed in the stereotypical outfit seen at Gasparilla. She was dressed in sweater and jeans. It was a cool night. We happened to catch each other's eyes, and we both did a double take.

She was in another car on the way to Gasparilla. We were all carpooling. So, I asked the crew that I was riding with, "Is the brunette taken?" They were like, "No, that's Denise. She just came out. She's a friend from one of my classes." I took a liking to her. This is how we first met. She's five years older than me, so that was one of the first things she asked me, "How old are you?" I was barely 21, but I said, "How old do you think I am?" She said, "how old do you think I am? You are 25, I think." I grinned and told her "Yeah, that's about right." I just left it at that, never told her the truth since I liked her. We hit it off. She wrote her number on a dollar bill with her lipliner. I still have that dollar bill to this day.

Meeting Denise became a key transition in my life. I was going to Italy, but I was kind of torn. I didn't really want to go to Italy now because I had just met Denise, but I still wanted the experience. I finally decided "this is the bee's knees, I'm an Italian guy, and I'm going to go see the Italian world."

I was so excited to see another country. I couldn't stop thinking about a gangster movie I watched with Keith. Keith had already been to Italy; he loves Italian heritage. He even has a business named Guido Fashions. He's all into this stuff. So, there I was, going to Italy, trying to find myself there. The only thing I was worried about is if I would give into Italian woman. I was dating Denise, and I really liked her, but I said that if I was living an Italian life, I needed to marry an Italian woman. That's what my thoughts were at the time. So, there I was over in Italy, though I didn't seek out anybody. If I happened to run into somebody, I was going to enjoy life and let things naturally develop.

I stayed about two and a half months with a guy from Brazil, and he would go out every night. He was with all the American women that were there. I was going to bed with a picture of Denise on my chest. I didn't have any desire to try to go out with him and kick it with the

American girls. I wanted it to be that if I met somebody, I'd simply met them. I'm glad that it didn't happen, at least not in that way.

I met a girl from Hungary and a lot of the American girls. I became friends with a lot of them and built up nice friendships. Some of them were cute, some of them were very attractive girls, but I told myself I had that A-personality, that winning mentality. I wasn't going to give in. I had plenty of opportunities, but I didn't.

We stayed in Umbria, which is the dead center of the country. We studied the Italian language. I'd go to class, and after class, we'd roam. Literally, we went to Rome. We even saw the Tower of Pisa. It was all a wonderful experience because I knew Italian, so it was easier to talk to folks. Because I had blonde hair, nobody would believe me when I told them I was Italian. I'd show my license with my last name, and then they would accept me. It was again that ego kicking in, and I would say, "No, I'm Italian, you know. And here's why..." Then when I talk in Italian, they'd say, "Okay." At that time, I felt like I was a star again.

The guy I was with, Ricardo from Brazil, he knew the language pretty well. He was Portuguese, and that's very similar to Italian. So, he and I hung out. While some other folks had to live with a family, we had an apartment by ourselves, so we could cook our own meals. While we were saving all our money there, others were going out to dinner every night because they didn't know how to cook.

Italy has so much to offer. We'd meet up with the groups and go to the Perugina factory, which is the chocolate factory, and the Bacis. We went to the Coliseum and the catacombs. I saw all these artistic pieces. I even met Newt Gingrich who was there as well; he gave me a big hug. Nobody recognized him. I gave him a hug on the street, and the people I was with said, "Who the hell was that guy?" I said, "That's Newt Gingrich." They kind of dawned on it, they're like, "Oh, the politician!" So, I had all these wonderful experiences. I even went to the Sistine Chapel. You name it, I saw it.

Florence was great as I would get great bargains simply for speaking Italian. Denise calls it 'Chichettoing It,' she can't understand how I can bargain with somebody. I got leather jackets for $100. They took me to the back of the store; it felt like something out of a Donnie Brasco movie. I went into the store, and they said, "Come on back. You're Italian." They'd take me into the back of the store and said, "Yeah, yeah, whatever you want." I was with Ricardo, and he spoke fluent Italian, so we were just killing it. We loved it; hopping on a train, going wherever we wanted. All the others were just trying to figure out where the Americans were. It was a great experience.
I grew up a lot during that trip because I saw my truth of people. How they acted no matter what color, what heritage, or what the situation was. The experience broke a lot of fears down inside me.

Being Catholic, I was interested in seeing a lot of the things in Italy because I had always heard about how St. Peter was buried under a Cathedral. It made it feel more real. I looked deeper into myself. I went six to ten feet down the ground into the catacombs, and I was able to feel the dust of the bodies that were there. There you could see that there was no discrimination. There were only real people. You saw a little casket that was for a kid, and then you saw the next dug out area was an adult, and it was very enlightening. I saw the statue of David and said, "Wow, that's from the 1500s." I saw it and realized how beautiful it is in person; the photos just do not do it justice. When you're looking at that, it's as you see it for what it is and then it starts to solidify some of the stories that you hear.

It goes back to what is truth? We need understanding.

In that particular moment of my experience, I began to tap into the spiritual side a little bit more. I was shifting gears and really started seeing myself rather than all the bigotry we talked about earlier. I started to drop a lot of my issues. I was starting to shed my outer skin. I still wasn't where I am today, but I was on that path. I started to review a lot, because I was associating the real stories now, with my hands touching the dirt of people that had died centuries ago. It kind of brought a different level of understanding to the story; rather than just looking into a book.

My uncle is a Priest, and he helped bring me into this era of my life. I had strength in my Catholic beliefs, which was now bolstered by my experiences in Italy. The churches and the Pope were what I needed to see. It was exactly where I needed to be at that time. It really opened me up to humanity. It wasn't just a fictitious world, like all we had in Florida, but you see that people are living over there and that there's a lot of culture. I would say the experience sparked my soul a little bit more because I could touch it.

> I am in love with every church
> And mosque
> And temple
> And any kind of shrine
> Because I know it is there
> That people say the different names
> Of the One God.
>
> - Hafiz poem "Would You Think it Odd?"

CHAPTER 6: AFTER ITALY

I came back from Italy wanting to share my experiences with everyone. The Professor actually asked me to stay in Italy and offered to help get me a job. I probably had $5 left because I bought all kinds of Italian jackets and shoes. So, there was a little fear again about how to manage my finances. I also had the desire to get back to Denise. I had these new feelings about how I'd touched life a little bit, and I wanted to share that and grow in the Catholic Church.

Although I was excited about the offer to stay in Italy, I was ready to return home. I wanted to see my mom and dad and get back to see Denise. I think Ricardo stayed a little bit longer, but he eventually also went home to Brazil.

When I arrived home, Denise and I got back together

again. We didn't lose touch. We went out a couple of nights after I had been back. I told her I loved her and she said it back. I thought 'this was the best thing ever' because I always had a fear of saying to somebody that I loved them. The only woman I had ever said that to before was my mother.

My belief growing up was, "if I'm going to say I love you, you damn sure better live up to the qualities of Mom." I was very close to mom, and I could tell her anything. I'd ask her, "Hey, what about this? What about that? Can you contract an STD if doing this and this?" Since this was my mom I was talking to; it got very personal. I didn't date many women because I was so close to my mom. She was everything, and she still is. She's still part of my life, but it was like I put her so high up on a pedestal, that I was closed off a lot to women when it came to dating. I dated a girl prior to Denise. When she told me she loved me, I said, "I don't love you. I'd say I love you but not like the love you're looking for. Like it's cool that we're dating, but I'm not ready to tell you that I love you." She asked me why, so I told her, "I'm putting you up next to my mother. I told my mother I love her."

This is yet another example of truth and paradigms. So that was a part of me, and here I was telling Denise that I love her. It was a big step for me. We grew close quickly after that. The day that I said, "I love you," there was a very strong connection, a very close bond.

Denise was there every step of the way and she never once questioned her decision to be with me. She's never judged me based around that. I'm so grateful that I came back to her, and that I didn't waste any time with other women. I always had a picture of her with me, and I sometimes would fall asleep with her on my chest. So, there was something there. When people talk about soul mates, I think that there's definitely a truth behind that.

However, life is difficult. Sometimes you feel you can't make it work, even if you are soulmates. There was even a time when I felt like I wanted to break away from Denise. I didn't think that I was going to marry her; I thought that was it. We both cried, but seemed always to have a desire to want to be around each other. Our relationship has driven my thoughts and my whole self for the better.

My marriage is a huge part of who I am every day. It's a relationship that continues to grow day after day. It's a feeling of love and compassion, a feeling of happiness and joy, even of equanimity. It encompasses all of the good words that you could probably throw out there. It's not something that is superficial.

After I got back from Italy, we knew that we were going to be together. We were driving back and forth between our apartments, not getting a lot of sleep. We thought this was stupid. We were both spending money on our apartments, and if we were serious about each other, then we could just make the commitment. So, we ended up moving into an apartment together and continued to grow closer together.

> Real magic in relationships means an absence of judgement of others.
>
> -Dr. Wayne Dyer

At the time, I was working as a valet attendant. I worked in the evenings; two nights a week. I was covering all my bills, but I was crazy busy.

I also had started coaching at USF on an internship in 2001. I was mainly focused on football, but I also worked with other sports. I did some women's basketball and cheerleading coaching. There was also a coach friend of mine, Ron, who had been around for a long time. He is a very successful guy. He was a strength coach at the University of Tennessee. He worked for special ops. He had a long resume and was much respected in the industry. I worked under him, along with two other guys. One guy, Graham, was working and he was in a similar boat as I was. He was getting paid but was still working on a degree. Then there was Travis. Travis was the number one assistant.

I worked there for two years, and it was a great experience. It opened me up to see that this was what I really wanted to do with my life. I had originally met Travis working as a personal trainer at Lifestyle Fitness. He worked there to offset his income. One day, we were talking about strength conditioning, and he mentioned that he coached and I said, "Man, I want to work as a coach. How do I get in?" He's like, "Well, I'm the assistant coach. You want to come down? I'll introduce you to Ronnie if that's okay." Ronnie and I were about the same age. At the time, he was probably the youngest strength coach out there. Like I said, he's been known for his hard work and his success.

When I worked at USF as a coach, we were training people in what we used to call "The dungeon." It was underneath the Sun Dome, the stadium at USF, and was about 2,000 square feet. So, we each coached five to six guys, and we were bumping shoulders in this cramped area. It wasn't the safest environment, but it was worth it. We made it work, and I learned a lot because of my go to, "I can do anything" attitude.

I was working as a coach during the day and still doing valet at night because it gave me the opportunity to begin at 5 o'clock. I worked with the guys at USF all day long. I would leave at about one in the afternoon, go home a little bit, take a little break and then drive off to work as a valet. That worked out for a little while until my stubbornness got in the way. I was asked to work at Channelside valeting one night. It was a slow night, and the owner of the company wanted everybody there to promote the business. I said, "I'm not going to make any money." I already saw how that was working and I said, "You're taking me away from the high paying location. This is bullshit." I meant every bit of what I said.

I made the decision to go that one night, but when they asked me, "Are you going to be here tomorrow? I said, "No, I'm not coming back tomorrow. I'm going to work at my other job because I didn't make $5 tonight." They said, "When you do that, you're going to get fired." I said, "Whatever." I went and worked that day, made the money I made and got fired. Then my buddy Ben, who I went to USF with, was working as a valet and I told him what had happened. He got me a job with him at Bern's. The rest was history, and I started working there. I loved that job. I got to work with a great friend. We spent most of our time laughing and kidding around. It was such a great time. It felt like we were little kids running around.

Then Ben and I started working out together. A couple of days a week, I would go and do my internship. It was such a good time in my life. I was just doing what I really liked to do.

From the internship, the plan was to work into coaching full time. I started to realize that it was the coaching that I loved, rather than the personal training. I was making some money in personal training, but I also had to valet because the personal training was something that I had to sell, which was a trade I hadn't learned yet. Working as a personal trainer at Lifestyles taught me how to sell. I was 22 years old and a strong guy, but I didn't know how to approach people.

Denise laughed at me. She's said, "You say hi to everybody." I replied, "I'll say hi to everybody on the streets. I'll talk to anybody. I'm not afraid of that." So, I'm not afraid to talk to people, but I wasn't able to get the number of clients I wanted. I wasn't making the money that I needed to make. The hard part for me to grasp was where to sell because I was thinking about what was best for my client, rather than thinking this is the service they want.

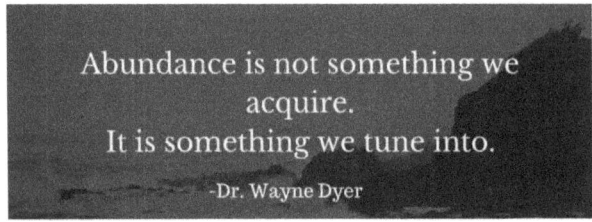

At the same time, Denise was working at TECO and finishing up her degree. Around the time of her birthday, we decided to get a dog. We bought a Boxer together as a couple, and that brought us even closer together.

So, at this stage of my life, I was working with Ben. I was having a good time working as a valet. It was such good money; I didn't want to break away from that. I also was having fun at USF because I was working with guys that I was friends with. I started to gain respect from the guys I coached because they saw me workout. I would teach them what I knew from my personal training experience, but also from my personal experiences in college playing football.

At my personal training position, there was a guy at the health club that I had sold a membership to. His name was Mike, and he was a very well-respected accountant. He has a couple of books out now. I started training him because he said he wanted to bench 300lbs. It was one of his goals even though he was 50 years old. He was very successful. He started his business in the early 80s and had done well. We became friends, and I got him to his 300-pound goal. So, at this point, I was building a friendship with him. I was working at USF, and I was still doing valet. My relationship with Denise was still going strong.

Then Mike started talking to me about business. I shared my idea with him that I wanted to take a CD and give that out to the people that I was training. I wanted to give them my workout to do at home. He said, "Why not take it globally? Put it on the world-wide web." I said, "What time tomorrow?" He said, "Well, bring me the CD." I showed him my idea, and I didn't have a non-disclosure agreement (NDA). It was just an honesty policy. I showed it to him. It was an automated thing that if you clicked on the person's arms, it would show your arm exercises; if you click on the legs, it will show your leg exercises; and so forth. I had trained a gentleman at USF who was good at programming software who helped me create the CD. I had the artistic background that came into effect when designing the visuals.

I put in all of these things in order to be successful, and here is the Law of Attraction that we talked about earlier. We were talking about projecting out what we want in our lives. I started to see how my life was beginning to pan out. Never would I have known it back then, of course. So, at this point, I was putting this stuff together, and Mike said he wanted to invest. He wanted to be a silent partner, and I said, "Great, let's do it."

We took the CD down to a place called Rapid Systems. It's a company that does software. They're big now and have satellites and internet services. But at the time they only focused on software development. So, Mike took his own money, which equated to almost $10,000 at the time, and we put it into action.

Because there was not a platform for Rapid Systems to run off, they didn't have enough information or enough of the knowledge to build the website. It was all new stuff, and it was a learning process as to how best to optimize it, and get the information onto a webpage. The webpage was to be designed whereby when people went on there they could simply fill out a medical questionnaire and click on what they needed to improve on. It would have been $20 a month. This system was to optimize my work, for example: if you had a physical problem, the questionnaire would negate the person's program, based on their previous injury.

Rapid Systems was spending a lot of time and money to build it. We had $10,000 invested into this thing, and we didn't even have a website up yet. It was something so new that nobody had ever done it before. They were trying to make it as automated as possible. Nobody knew how to build it. We were spending all this money, effort, and time. Seven people were working on the project to build it the way I wanted it. The entire program was based around the client; it didn't have to entail me at all. That was clever back then, and now it is something everybody does. The best way you can optimize a business is by streamlining it. To utilize your time effectively as possible.

However, because of all the problems and setbacks, we had to pull the plug on it. It was Mike's call because he didn't know what, if anything, the next $10,000 was going to accomplish. Some years later, we saw that Oprah funded a very similar layout with a guy by the name of Jorge Cruz, he did it from a diet perspective, though. When you type in all of your information, you can get a personalized diet.

Mike owned a complex in town that he allowed me to go in and build a workout facility. This was a way that I would try to bring back some of the losses he had spent.

I had left USF at that time and was trying to branch off to do this. I was working hard at night and was still working at Lifestyles. I had a good income coming in, but I didn't have enough. During the day, I was doing installations of the gym equipment. I was slowly getting away from the late nights because I wanted to spend my weekends with Denise, so I moved away from the valet. This allowed me to make my own gym. Mike gave me the room to do it, and we built it. I called it Smart Fit Sports and Fitness Clinic.

I was on top of the world again because I was getting to do something I had always dreamt about. I had my own business. It became the next big step in my life. I was pursuing my career and seeing all parts of my life coming together.

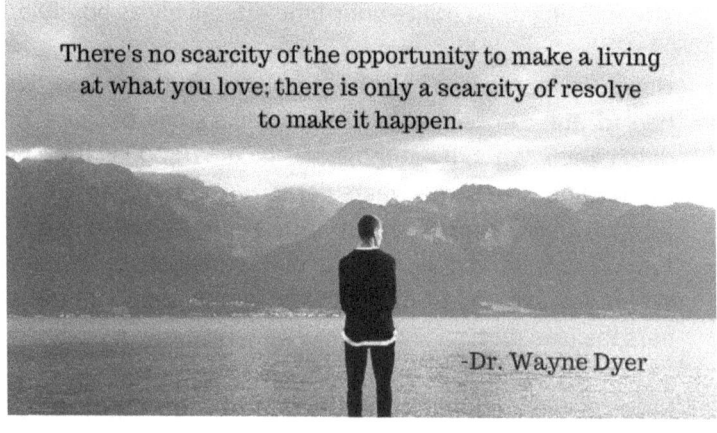

CHAPTER 7: STARTING A BUSINESS

It took 18 months to get Smart Fit Sports and Fitness Clinic up and running. I finally got it started after I bought equipment online, through Craigslist, and bought the flooring through Busy Body. It was similar to piecing a puzzle together. I did an open house and had the Army put up a rock climbing wall. The only issue with the building was we weren't able to put up any big signs because of the association's rules.

The location was right at a major intersection. Without any signs out to advertise the place, I wondered how I would be able to attract traffic? I didn't have any clientele because I was only working through word of mouth.

I was only 25, still pretty young, and I didn't have exactly know-how to progress. Mike was guiding me as a mentor/partner. I think that if you're around a skilled mentor, it's quite easy to progress along the correct path. In this case, being young and not knowing how to make money, I was influenced by a gentleman who said one way to make money is to run your own business. I was bitten by the entrepreneur bug. Once you have been bitten, it's hard not to scratch that itch.

Prior to this point in my life, I had tried to follow my Dad's route of gaining a good education and getting a reliable job. My dad is very bright. If there was any question in regard to history or English, he was the guy to go to. He went to law school, but he never suggested running my own business. He always said, go to school and get an education. I think sometimes we forget education can come from different sources. Some of the most influential business people don't even have a high school degree. Our society has told us that we must go to an institution, pay money and gain a degree in order to become successful. We believe that if you want to make money, you need to be educated.

Mike had other business partners that were with him, and he owned a CPA branch that he was influenced by as well. In 2004, he was showing me the business and mentoring me, but I was still had questions. He told me I had to go to seminars and talk to others to learn. But I still wasn't awake enough to know how simple it could be. When we talk about the Law of Attraction, it only works if you put it into practice. You can't just sit there, close your eyes, and think it's going to happen. Although, I think it's very possible it can happen that way. It would take, however, someone who is willing to go and meditate for twenty-fours a day. But you still must put some type of practice and effort in meditating. So, I found myself wanting to work, but I wanted to do it in such a way that it would bring me prosperity, which I had never known previously in my life due to my upbringing. I don't blame my parents. Society has driven all of us to think that we're not allowed or entitled to have success.

I felt that it was a great experience for me, but it was also a difficult time as I was at the mercy of others. I still wanted to do certain things, but because it wasn't my money, my options were limited. At some point, they'd say, "no you can't get any additional money." So that was tough, and I was still trying to find my way. I was crawling up a little bit, going up to the Chamber of Commerce and meeting people. I wasn't afraid of that; it's just that I didn't know the in's and out's yet. I was just getting my feet wet, and I didn't know what to do. I think that was the biggest challenge. This beginning slump lasted probably about 12 to 18 months or so. I picked up some clients here and there, and I was putting a little bit of money in my pocket. I had enough money to have food to eat and to get enough to get to and from work.

However, I never knew if it would be enough to cover expenses and bills. Mike was driving the business side of things, so I was very fortunate to have him. He was such a wonderful part of my life, and I'm still friends with him to this day. He gave me the benefit of his experience, and I was kind of oblivious to it. I was good at what I knew, but I still had a lot to learn. Mike acted as my mentor with the business aspect. We would have meetings and talk, but, beyond that, it was more or less on my own.

Mike mentored me. He introduced me to some of his friends, those who were training, including some of his business partners. Of course, I also met his wife, and we had a friendship, but there weren't enough people that I was invited to meet or network with. He told me how he did it, through speaking engagements and getting around, but it wasn't as easy as I thought it would be.

If I had not been on the sports side of things, I probably would have thought a little differentially. I was still doing the personal training; I had no problem saying, "Hey I'm opening my own place." I had a one-minded thought towards USF. I was a training coach, I was trying to open a business, but I was also still a personal trainer on the side at Lifestyles. So, I knew how to sell, but I didn't know how to connect them. I didn't know how to put all the skills into play to make things work; I wasn't ready for that.

My buddy Napoleon called me up one day and said, "Hey, I want to see if you're interested in working with me with the Rangers." (This was the Texas Rangers major league baseball team.) I said, "Well, I just opened a business you know. If you don't mind, can I call you back?" I was excited about it, but I also had this obligation to the business.

There was nothing that was going to come between me trying to get Mike some of his money back. The little bit of investment that I put forward, including the equipment, painting the walls and that kind of stuff, it was just sweating equity. Then, of course, he covered the electric bill, the internet and other expenses like that. So, there I was faced with a question, 'what do I do?'

An offer was made to work for a Minor-League level with a Major League level kind of hybrid. The job would entail a lot of help coordinating the Major League players that would come in for rehab and for offseason in Arizona, so there was a long-disabled timeframe. They would go to Arizona in most circumstances if there was something that they weren't able to do in Texas.

I was excited because I've always been a big baseball guy. Major League baseball was very appealing at this point. Finally, decided that the job sounded great. My business wasn't going as well as I thought that it would, based around the mentoring that I was having. I was being coached to be this entrepreneur-type mentality, but I still didn't quite understand it. I was oblivious and blind to what I was doing. All I thought was "build it, and they'll come," but they weren't coming.

Napoleon flew down, and we met, and he said, "Do it for three months and see if you like it." When he first told me, it was real fresh. I had known Napoleon from USF. He and I worked together. He landed a job with the Texas Rangers Baseball. I was just honored that he thought of me. So, he flew down, and we met over dinner and talked about the job, and I got excited. Denise even said, "Oh, you've' definitely got to do it. It's Major League Baseball. It's something you've got to do." And I said, "Yeah, but I'll be away from you for three months." She's like, "Yeah, but it's just three months of our lives. Who cares? Just go and do it." It made me feel better about taking the job, but I couldn't just leave yet.

Denise had a great job. She was still working at TECO, so she was able to cover a lot of our finances at home. The business was going downhill so fast. It was either time for me to move on or Mike was going to pull the plug. It felt like that all the time. We had been in business about a year at this point.

About 18 months later, Napoleon called me on the phone and asked if I was ready to go work with him. So, I went to Mike, and I told him what was going on, and I said, "Listen, I don't know how you feel about the business, but I haven't brought in enough." Mike was really cool about my new job offer. He didn't ask for any money from me. He didn't take a dime. I told him, "You know I've got to go off and get a job. This business isn't working." He understood. So, it wasn't as scary as I thought it was going to be.

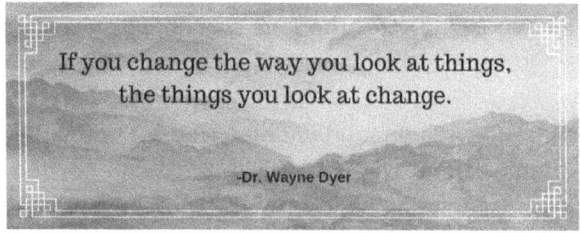

If you change the way you look at things, the things you look at change.

-Dr. Wayne Dyer

So, we just shut it down. I sold the equipment off, put it all on Craigslist, then somebody came and bought all the flooring. Then I used that money for my drive to Arizona. I drove out and stayed at Napoleon's house. He gave me one of his spare bedrooms, and I stayed there with him for three and a half months.

At the end of the three and a half months, he said to me, "What are you thinking?" I replied, "I thought this was a great opportunity. I had a good time." I saw a lot of different perspectives on baseball that I hadn't seen before. I had a new-found respect for the Major Leagues because the talent level was just amazing. I would go out and train with young guys. Some of them were just getting ready to turn 17 or 18 years old. They were throwing 96-97mph fastballs. It was a pro-level experience.

I helped with rehab to strengthen and condition, which would be running or weightlifting, or anything in that realm. At this stage in my life, I had done it for quite a few years. So, I walked in with that I was going-to-kick-everybody's-ass type of attitude. At the beginning of my three months, they gave me my gear and everything I needed to know to get started on my first day. I walked in, and Napoleon introduced me to some people. He introduced me to my first assignment, a player who had been in the Major Leagues for 16 years. That's a long time to be in the Major Leagues. He was with the Rangers organization when I got there, and he was doing rehab, "Go ahead and take him through. They need ab work." I went into this little training room where I had a Major leaguer and a couple of other Minor League players. I said, "Alright, this is what we're going to do."

Bruce said, "I'm not doing that." I didn't know how to react to that. I asked, "What do you mean you're not going to do it?" I thought everybody would just do it. I was used to that at USF. 'Why are you here then, if you're not going to do it?' That's the way my mind was going. The A-personality type kicked in a little bit. I started to get a little irritated, but I thought maybe he was just messing with me. However, he was serious. He told me, "You know what; I'm going to run in the morning. I want you to run with me. All you have to do is make the entire run. The only thing I ask is that you don't stop running. If you make the full run, I'll do it. Anytime you ask me to do anything; I'll do it for you." I replied, "What kind of run are you talking about?" He smirked, "Oh, it's only about two miles."

I hadn't run in years, and I wasn't used to the damn 115-degree weather. So, the next day he's running with me, and we're running at my pace. I made it the whole way, but he blew past me during the last 800 meters. He just took off. The whole thing was a sign of respect. I think at that level people don't want someone telling them what to do if they aren't of a similar physical level.

While I was at USF, one of the things that the strength coach, Ronnie, said was you either have to out-lift the players, out-perform them, or you have to outsmart them. You have to continue with your education. It dawned on me while I was running. It was right here in front of me! I was the new dog in the pack, just coming in.

When we went back, he didn't do the exercises that day, but the other guys did. They performed the ab workout that I made for them. He did do it the following day. All it took was me not stopping. Two miles out there was tough to do, and I was running it. It wasn't just jogging. He was setting the pace, but you could tell that he could have left me at any time. The guy was in shape. I got my feet wet quickly.

I was working with rehab guys at first and then when rookie ball players started to show up, took those guys as well. A typical day would start with Minor League level. They would come in and get breakfast. I'd work out first. Then we would do some field work. I'd take them through the team stretch, and then the players would go and do whatever they needed to do. Next was the pitchers. I would have them run and finish their workouts. Then I'd go up and train the rest of the team in the weight room. I would take them through a program suitable for the athletes in their level.

We'd work side by side with the athletic trainers and then go according to with the problems the players were individually having. The pitchers were pissed that I would make them run. That was always a battle. They always felt like, "Man, I'm in rehab. I don't need to do this. I'm just here to throw."

I learned the ways of training baseball players within those three months. I could fine the players if they didn't show up for the weight room. Some of them were coming to America for the very first time. They would get in and start working out. They were very receptive, and they did very good work with me. However, some of the older guys that were there rehabbing, they would influence them. They would start to see what they could get away with. Like children pushing the boundaries.

It was a great experience for the first three months. It was similar to being this boot camp leader with guys that don't even know English. It was all very interesting. I tried to learn Spanish, and I was quick on my feet with that, especially the body parts. In return, I got to teach them stuff.

Most of the guys from the Dominican Republic had a third-grade education. They'd literally be pulled out of school at a young age and live in a baseball training compound that was regulated by some of the major sports agents. They would feed them, provide clothes, and give them all their gear. But if a player signed with a team, they would take an extravagant percentage. They would take 35-40% of a signing bonus.

However, the kids probably wouldn't have had a chance

otherwise because their parents were poverty-stricken. So, they would take these kids, train them how to play baseball and then the organization would give them a tryout. They usually tried out at 13 or 14 years old, and if they make it, then there's interest from a Major League club. They would feed them and keep them at the complex. Every Major League team has a system like this.

The compound was located in the Dominican Republic. They had two fields with all the equipment. It was protected by guards that carried semi-automatic weapons. It was insane when I was down there. They are farming these young kids. During their training, they were not getting an education. They were specifically just teaching baseball. The kids were playing games, and they were getting better. However, they could get cut, too, just like any other sport. If a new 13 or a 14-year-old kid comes in, and he's outperforming the others, this meant someone else was out. Some kids would get homesick and they would run away from the complex. There was a dining hall where they had cafeteria ladies and guys to take care of the players. There was a weight room down there as well. I had the opportunity a few years into the job to fly down there. I helped set up the weight room and one of the guys that I worked with, he'd come up for the spring training and help out, but he was stationed down there. He was a great guy. He was from Panama. You had to be creative with those kids because you see them every day and they live there. It's a totally different way of life; they're basically locked into the place.

The compound had bunk beds that would house between six or eight kids in one room. You'd be on a property, and then adjacent to that property was another Major League team that was covered with trees. They wouldn't want the other team to see te upcoming kids who could play. It was a very secluded place. They wouldn't let you on the campus unless you were a part of the Rangers or another team. They were trying to discover who's going to be the next Major Leaguer.

They weren't paying the families anything. The kids were there in the hope that they were going to get on a team one day. So, the agents would bring the kids from wherever they found them. They would house them from when they were in third grade until they were 13 or 14. They'd take them over to their contacts and walk them on the field, "Hey, we want to try out this kid here." The Rangers would have scouts look at them, and they would say yes or no. If scouts liked them, then the Rangers at that point would start housing them and paying for what they needed. They still wouldn't be under a fully-fledged legal contract until they were 18. So down there, I know they were still getting some type of return for working out and practicing. They were not getting paid, but they were getting all their housing and food paid for by the Rangers.

So, after the first three months, I came back to Florida and told Mike that I was done with the business that I needed to take this job. At the time, it was only the Rangers and three other baseball clubs out of the 32 baseball teams that had full-time positions like this. All the other clubs were doing internships. There were paid internships, but you can't live off the little compensation. At this point, the three months had been a paid internship, but then I was offered a full-time position. I told Denise, and she was really excited for me. She's told me to take the job because she wanted to move. She wanted a new experience too.

The 2007 era was when I started a full-time position with the Major League baseball because that was when spring training started back up. By this point, I had met all kinds of new people. Spring training was an interesting and exciting time. I liked working spring training a lot. If I could have *just* worked spring training, I would have. It was a great time because 250 guys were there; coaches were there, and everybody meets at this one place. A lot of times you'd go out to dinners, and there are multiple meetings to attend.

You build a great rapport with folks. In the beginning, it was even more exciting because it was so new, different, exciting on the job and in our personal lives. We moved to a new home every few months. We were excited with the idea that we're going to be away from the same old town and family. This whole new perspective was what we hoped we needed at the time.

CHAPTER 8: ARIZONA

In my second year of working with the Major League and Minor League players, the idea of forming a new identity was something I still couldn't shake off. Now it was spring training again, a lot of guys liked me because I had pushed them hard in the weight room; from my football background, I trained them hard.

At Murray State, out of 110 guys, I was one of the strongest guys on the entire team. I knew how to work; I knew how to motivate. I knew how to push people, and I still do. However, at that time in my life, I was yelling and screaming to get my point across. I think this really started my downward spiral. Everything that I was doing was an energy source for my life. If you're constantly putting in negative energy, that's what you get out. Not knowing this at the time, I thought that being negative all the time was just a way of life. It had become what I call my survival teaching.

It was like a high. I was telling people what to do like I was the boss. In actuality, I was ruining my life, and I didn't know it. I was oblivious to it. I didn't know that it was having such a big effect on me. I was still 'asleep.' I didn't have the awakening factor just yet.

I was really busy too. It was all work and no play. I didn't even see Denise much. I did see her during the first year some, but the second year being in 'Frisco, I didn't see her at all. I was on the road a lot. I was in a hotel 70 days out of a year that I was coaching. Meaning, out of 160 games, 70 of them I would spend in a hotel. They would say you get two days off, but I'd come off the bus, and it would be 3:00 in the morning after a long bus ride. So, I'd sleep most of the day. In reality, I only got a half of day off; then I'd do a full day again. I would train the guys all morning, and then be at the game until late at night. The days I did have off, I would spend with Denise, just loving each other. We had a good time. We'd go to dinner and spend quality time together.

After a while, it did start to a cause a strain on our relationship. I was stuck in the external way of thinking at that point. I was just in survival mode. I thought that this was the only way. I had spent my entire existence searching for my identity. I know now what that was, it's clearer to me now. However, at the time I was lost. My experiences were building up to what I do now. During my fifth year in it, I was at my wit's end.

Even though I was pretty much on my own during the season, which I enjoyed, I was getting bogged down. I had to motivate guys every day, and it was wearing me out. For example, the pitchers had to do a certain amount of running. This was a coaching group decision. However, in the middle of the season, when it was 100 degrees out, they just didn't want to run anymore. They'd complain and moan about it. It was dragging my morale, patience and overall happiness down.

It didn't help that I always had to answer to somebody. I have never liked reporting to someone or being told what to do. I had a cool hitting coach when I was working in California, and he stuck up for me because he saw the value in the fitness side of things. Now I had to write a report every two weeks on how these guys were progressing. So, if they were doing well or if they were doing badly, I'd still have to write about them. I think that stressed me out a little bit. I didn't realize it because I was already in too deep. I was the guy that they were all looking at. If they were reading this, it would affect whether they were going to return next year for a job. That was kind of like, "This guy is cool to me. How should I write this? But also, be honest about, Hey, you know what, he's cool, but he's a turd." Some of that was tough because I felt like there were two sides to every player: one day I'd see him, and he's doing okay, and then the next day he wouldn't show up for the weight room, so I have to write that in the report.

As an authority figure, I was asked to report on them. It was tough because I was living with these people as well. I was on the road with them. I was living in a hotel with them, and everybody's personality is different. There was always somebody on top of you about whether or not you were doing the right thing. All of this was going on while I was trying to hold down some sort of a personal life. I would go to the ballpark, go home, or go to the hotel. It was necessary to feed these guys as well. At the end of the night, we had to come up with a good healthy way to get them nourished with fruit or snacks. During the day, I had to look over their protein intake, so we were ordering in protein bars or protein powders and then their supplementation, whether or not somebody could use it or not use it. It was just another thing to worry about.

I was working side by side with the athletic trainers, too. A lot of them were cool, but I had to help them out with the laundry and move all their bags. Players and coaches would get off the bus and go in the hotel, go to sleep. The trainer and I, however, would have to go to the park and unload their shit, including coaches' stuff. The trainer and I would have to go to the park and unload their baggage, including coach's stuff. In the Major League, they have clubbies to do that. Clubbies take care of bags, laundry, food and such. It was exhausting. After a full day, all I wanted to do was go to bed. I didn't want to move 25 players and the coach's stuff while everybody else was going to sleep. I was starting to get irritable now at this point because I felt they were not paying me enough to do all this.

On top of everything else, I also became their counselor. Some guys would come in and tell me about their ex-girlfriends that they just had a fight with, that they had to break up, or about something that was going on in their life. We'd get close to each other, like brothers. But also, I was this fatherly parent too, "Do the right thing man, get your running done." In the later years when all of this continued to pile up, it became overwhelming. Working with the same guys all of the time, they start to see your soft side. I was caring and not always the asshole. I couldn't be in their face all the time, especially for four years. It would have been too hard to maintain that. So, at that point, I was starting to build a rapport with some of the players. I'd meet some of the veterans, and people that had been around me, and who I'd seen at spring training. All season I would be out there training the players in the off-season, too. That's a lot of time I was spending with them and getting to know them. They would get to know me too, and they learned that I was just as much a human as they were. There was no reason for us to fear each other.

At this point in time, I was really starting to find my feet. My personality was leveling out a little bit, but that's because I did the job for four years straight. I think closer to that fifth year is when it really became taxing. After all that build-up that I experienced, I had a panic attack on an airplane. It was my dad's 70th birthday, and we were in Texas. It was time to go home and see him. I hopped on a plane and Denise, and I was flying home for the weekend. I got on the plane, and typically, from the Catholic upbringing, I would always say my Hail Mary's or Our Fathers. After I had said my little prayer, I had a panic attack. Denise was like, "You don't look so good" I said, "I don't feel so good." I didn't know what caused it; I just started feeling claustrophobic.

The next thing I knew, I was in the damn doctor's office trying to figure out what happened. That year was a tough year returning to baseball. Previously I talked about the power of the law of attraction or self-fulfilling prophecies. I got exactly what I was asking for.

I sat in the corner of a spare bedroom of my house crying and telling Denise who was pregnant at the time with our first baby, that I did not want to go back to work because I was fearful of experiencing another panic attack. If anybody has experienced a panic attack, they make all of the thoughts you're having feel more real than reality. It's like the world is caving in all around you and there's nothing you can do about it.

The problem is they're all just driven by irrational thoughts. The irrational thoughts turn into an adrenaline rush, and then the adrenaline rush just goes back to the thoughts, creating an endless cycle. I am sure everyone has experienced a type of panic at some time in their lives. Whether it was a parent who can't find their kid at the shopping mall for a quick moment; or almost having an accident driving; or even getting pulled over by the police. Science tells us that this is the fight or flight response. This is natural for us to survive.

My panic attacks turned into this irrational lifestyle and caused me to zone out. I had no idea what was happening. I didn't have them a lot; I just had a lot of irrational thoughts. I usually got the panic attacks when I had to get on the bus. I was prescribed Xanax. I would take it to try to calm down, but I didn't want to because it didn't feel right. I still took it, however, because it was the only way I'd get on the bus. I'd take it an hour or so before I had to get on a bus and I'd pop a couple extra right before because it was the only way I could manage things.

It wasn't just the bus either. If I was on a bus or a plane, that's when I had to take it because I felt claustrophobic and I had these irrational fears come from me. I never had problems on planes before, but then I did; all because of that first time.

I've tried to figure out what could have caused that first panic attack. The only thing I could think of was a fear of death. I had a fear moment because I thought of my dad and how I would miss my dad if he died because at the time he was 70 years old. I was sad because I wasn't able to see my family as much anymore. I'd been gone for five years at that point, which seemed to have passed quickly.

My grandmother also died during that time, and I wasn't able to go home for the funeral. My mom said, "Don't worry, were just going to do a little quick thing." I told myself it didn't really matter, but I think it did take a toll on me because of where my mind was at that point in my life. Even if it were just her ashes, I never got a chance to say goodbye to her. I felt regret for allowing myself to put my baseball job as a higher priority than family. I kept telling myself, "Oh I'm in the middle of a season." And I made the mistake of staying with the team even when Napoleon would have been cool with me leaving. He told me "If you need to go, you need to go." He wasn't forcing me to stay there, but I didn't feel that way. I would have felt weak if I left because I had already made the idea in my mind that I was this tough guy and tough guys are not supposed to cry over anything. It just made me feel weak and nervous. I knew people would have understood that I had to go home.

People play baseball, they lose their folks, and life goes on. But for whatever reason, I kept that tough guy mentality that was in my mind. So, I didn't go home and then a couple months later it was my dad's birthday. It was this big surprise birthday, and my brother Peter had gotten a limousine, and we went over to a place in Orlando for dinner. It was a Brazilian steakhouse. As we were getting into the limo, I had another panic attack.
I just felt claustrophobic. This was right after the plane incident. We got off the plane, got to Winter Haven and I told my mom. My mom has suffered from anxiety, depression, and panic attacks for years. So, I recognized the symptoms.

There was one particular instance that I remember vividly of my mom having a panic attack. We boys would always argue about who was sitting where in the car and who was sitting in the front seat. We went out to dinner, and instead of hearing us argue, my mom would just give up the front seat. She was cool about it. One time, she got in the backseat, and she became claustrophobic. She kept yelling, and everyone said, "What the hell is going on with you, mom?" and nobody knew.

I think she was suffering from it back then and I didn't know about it. Of course, now I know. When I got on the plane, the panic attack had built up from being broken down by the stress levels of my job for four years. There I was with the idea that I was going to die. I freaked out on the damn plane. I couldn't catch my breath. We had a layover in Houston. It was a short flight from Arlington to Houston, then from Houston to Tampa. So, when we got on the other plane, we were the first passengers to get on. I got to my seat, and I started having another panic attack. Denise kept saying, "Just sit down and relax." I had a PSP which was a portable Play Station. She's suggested, "Just play that damn game of yours." So, I sat down and played the game, and it took my mind off of it, I thought that I was doing okay. Then right before takeoff, I freaked out again.

I tried going to the bathroom. They're not supposed to let you, but they stewardess said, "We're flying." I persisted, "I got to go." And she finally caved in, "Well, you're on your own." I said, "That's fine, just get out of my way, I've got to go to the bathroom." I went to the bathroom, and just looked in the mirror and threw water on my face to calm me down. It felt like I couldn't breathe. I went back to my seat and made it through the flight. I got home, and then told my mom; she said she had been dealing with it for several years. She gave me something to help me calm down.

I found out my brother John had suffered with it as well. He had already been diagnosed and had been given Xanax. So, there I was and I said, "Mom, you know, I'm kind of freaking out about getting in that damn limo a little bit." I was okay; I got to the restaurant. Then when I got to the restaurant, I was sitting around the table. As my body got full of food, I had that kind of bloated feeling. It made me think I couldn't breathe. So, I walked outside, my mom came out, took my pulse. She said, "You're fine, and you're just having a panic attack again."

I slept it off once we got back to my folk's place. I wrapped my mind around the whole thing and then I was freaking out because I had to fly back. I had to get to Texas; I had to get back because this was an all-star break. All I kept thinking was, "how the hell am I going to do that?" My mom was the one who gave me something to relax on the plane. She instructed, "Here, just take these. You'll be fine, get back on the plane."

Denise and I got on the plane, I took the medicine, and I was fine. I went back to work. We were done with baseball, so instead of going to Texas, we were flying to Arizona because of the spring training. Denise went back to Texas because we had Cujo the Boxer dog and I flew back to Arizona to see Nap. He didn't know about the panic attacks or what I was experiencing. But I had told one of my close friends, the trainer, about what I was experiencing. He asked, "Well, do you want to go see the doctor?" And I agreed, "Yeah, can you get me an appointment?" It was easy for the team doctor to see me.

So, I went to the doctor, and the doctor I saw had actually told me that she had experienced it. I was confused. "What the hell is going on? Everybody's getting panic attacks." She explained, "I can get you Xanax to help calm you down." She did a thorough run-up to make sure everything was good. I just assumed that it was panic attacks. It was hard taking Xanax just to get through the season. I didn't mind taking them during the bus ride.

After the anxiety had started, I began to experience depression because I was found myself feeling afraid and insecure of everything. The job was part of it. I feared small little things that you would never think about normally. For example, I would see cracks on the road and think that the damn Earth was going to split open. If anybody's ever experienced it, it was like everything, and anything made me fear death, and I thought that I was going to die. It was just insane.

The best explanation that I can give is from the external environment, the paradigms that we're in are nothing but memories. The panic attacks just go around whatever your thoughts are. I kept having thoughts of fear that something bad was going to happen to me. Even driving in the car sometimes gave me this feeling. I couldn't come to grips with the fact that I was going to die someday, even though I was this healthy young buck at the time. I just couldn't get past the idea that I was going to die.

I was obsessed with dying, obsessed with the idea that it was going to actually happen to me like I was the only one that was going to beat it. Life is awesome. I think that these thoughts come back to the spoiled mentality. I had the idea, a sort of entrapped mentality, where I felt like I couldn't go anywhere now that I had this job. I kept thinking "What am I going to do next?" I felt that this superficial mentality I had, still wasn't strong enough to get me what I wanted.

I was happy, but not 100% happy. I wasn't fulfilled. I wanted things to happen right away for me. I wanted to be the next coordinator or some other higher position. I wanted more. I wanted to be the next Major League strength conditioning coach. I think that was a big part of it. I didn't have it; I didn't understand why.

It was wonderful, at first. I was on a big high. And then all of a sudden, I started fearing everything based on this irrational thinking. I set myself up with a lot of good guys, and because they are my friends now, I felt like, "damn, where's my opportunity now? What am I going to do next?" I think part of it too is that you see the money aspect of it when you're around the Major League players. Even Minor League players were making tons of money. They're not making much from the level that they're playing at, but if they're projected to be in the Major League, they might have been given a large signing bonus. I saw guys that got $4 million signing bonus. People and pitchers would come in and would have $2 million signing bonus. I was around guys that were Major Leaguers in spring training and would pull up in a Lamborghini. I felt that I was working on these guys, keeping them in shape to play, and I was getting paid jack crap. I wondered when life was going to give me the break I felt I deserved?

I'd been hustling for five years, doing all this stuff and I felt I was still looked down upon. I think that's where a lot of it started to hit, too. It just built up and brought a lot of that negative energy to my body.

I wanted to start making some money and living a normal life. I didn't want to be on the roller coaster any longer. I felt like that's what it was. It was like two days out of a month; I got a day off. Then I got one month off completely from the organization, which felt like it wasn't anything at all.

I missed my family. I was at a point in my life where I just felt burnt out and didn't have enough of what I wanted. That was the other side of things. There were a lot of policies that drove me, one of them being the clubhouse. In the clubhouse, there was a policy that you had to tip your clubbies, but if you didn't tip your clubbies a certain amount, then you didn't get anything. Clubbies are the clubhouse managers, they are kind of the gatekeeper to your success, and frankly, it's kind of shady. They know all the big wigs. They take care of the interior of the clubhouse. They make sure it's clean. Not all of them have to do all the janitorial work, but there are some that have to. Some of the guys that have been there a long time, they make the younger guys clean. So, they hire these younger guys to do that the cleaning. The clubbies have to wash all the clothing, the jerseys, and they're responsible for all the gear. They have a big job.

My egotistical mindset was to say, "That's not your money, that's the organization's money, let me get a pair of shorts." And they're like, "Well, tip me. If you don't tip me, then you don't get the shorts." That's how it was.

I went to the general manager one time and told him I'm having trouble with this particular clubby. I'd say, "What's the deal with this? I'm new to baseball. I'm not that new now that I'm kind of in-synch here, but what're your thoughts?" And his answer was, "If my wife knew how much money I give to clubbies each year she wouldn't understand it either." That was a kind of "under the bus, leave it alone, don't go down that road" response. That's kind of what my hint was, but I'd fight that because I felt like this wasn't right.

I'll give you an example; one clubhouse manager got fired when I was there. He was with the Major Leagues for quite some time. When he was with Texas, he got a check for $275,000 as a tip. I saw that there were not just a few dollars here and there, there's some shady stuff going on, and that's the way baseball is; that won't change. I think this was when I started really having that internal struggle because I thought, 'these jerks are getting paid $500,000. I'm working a crazy amount of hours more than he is, yet I'm not getting paid shit.' And I can't even get a pair of underwear from the guy. I'm like, "Let me get a pair of sliders." And the answer would be "no." I would respond, "Dude, it's not your sliders, so don't tell me I can't have them." They responded, "You never played in the Major Leagues," so it wasn't always pleasant.

I'll give you another example. My fourth year, I almost went toe to toe with a pitching coach. When I say almost, it was very close. In fact, the pitching coach got fired that year. Of course, I got fired at the end of the year, but I made it through the entire year first. They had to escort him out of the clubhouse because they thought that we were going to fight. Then we got back; he and I squared up. It's a weird industry. I suppose because you go to work and at the end of the night everybody's drinking and acting like your buddy. It didn't seem like a job. It felt like a brotherhood, and we were just going to play baseball.

Anyway, we got in this argument over a baseball player, and at this point, we had a new owner. I had a good relationship with him, and he saw us as a very valuable asset to baseball because he worked out as well. So, the strength conditioning guys were starting to build their name up, when he came in. We were on the up that year, and the pitching coach that had come in didn't believe that strength conditioning was very important. There happened to be one of the prospects that I was working with that assisted him. So, there would be a pitching coach conflict that said, "This is my player." I said, "He's all of ours. We all are only going to make him better."

He, of course, didn't like that. Then we said some words and argued a little bit. Then there was a time when we had gotten our ass kicked, 14 to two. It was really bad; it wasn't the best time, but I picked a battle anyway. In this battle, I wasn't going to lose because I felt strong about the strength conditioning program. Like I said, I already told you that the club was making money and I thought "Where the hell is our respect?"

So, there we were battling. It was a great year, but then the pitching coach was totally smashing the program. I felt it was my place to go to bat. When I went to bat for the strength conditioning role, they fired him. Not over me, but because he had already burned his bridges with some of the other coaches. But we almost had a fight right there, two grown men. We closed the door so that none of the players would see it. We were in the coaches' office, I stood up, and he stood up. We were getting to toe to toe, and then the manager and hitting coach got in between us. I said, "Let's go if you want to go. I don't care." I was ready, but it never escalated that far. This situation only added to the stress of the job.

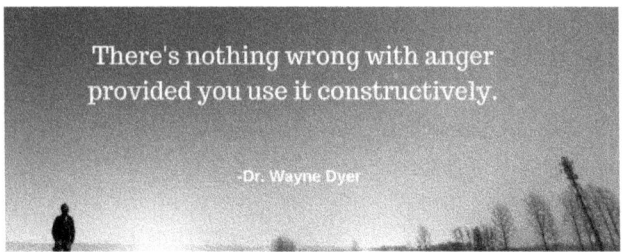

I always had to mop the floor. The janitorial people didn't do the weight room for some reason. So, when I'd go in, I'd really clean it and make sure it was sanitary. One day, this player came in and said, "Damn, this place looks clean." I said, "Thanks. I'm trying to keep it this way. That's why I tell you guys in spring training not to wear your spikes in here and stuff. Respect the way the room is because I'm the one who's cleaning it." So, he spat on the floor and rubbed it with his foot.

This was behind the scenes; it happened all the time. They were able to say whatever they wanted to us. They could be disrespectful. What was I supposed to do? Would I fight with a 25-year-old even though he was only a couple of years younger than me? I grew up fighting so I had this urge to defend my right be respected. However, I was a grown up and had to act professionally. That was a lesson that I had to learn; how to control myself and not react to every little thing that happened.

I was losing control of players, and I was losing control of myself. I was turning into a jokester; a having fun type of guy. When I was at spring training people saw me, because they had built a rapport with me. I was the same guy for three or four years. It's natural to build a rapport with them. I couldn't be a hard ass all the time. Things were going really good, and I felt that I was part of this institution finally.

Then out of nowhere I was let go and had to start all over again. I lost my job and had a new baby to care and provide for.

The anxiety was overwhelming. Everything crumbled away. All the wonderful things that happened to me seemed minuscule. Otherwise, I wouldn't be here writing this book, and I wouldn't be telling stories of how to try to get out of things when you are in too deep.

CHAPTER 9: NFL

After baseball, life was tough for a while. I had no job, a wife who had given up her high-paying career to follow me into baseball, a new baby, and a mortgage. Unemployment is not enough to live off. On top of all this, I had the anxiety and depression.

Things started to turn around when I was offered a job at BayCare and a chance to work with the NFL. This particular BayCare location handled rehab and also had a wellness center. The wellness center ran a gym, where basically anyone could pay and work out. They had the same equipment as any other gym. I told Denise that it sounded like a great opportunity. They had benefits, and I would be doing what I liked to do. All I had to do was to sell personal training to folks. Denise was concerned and said, "Yeah, but you've got to drive to St. Petersburg." I said, "I don't care. I'm going to take the job." It was about an hour and a half away from our home.

I was so excited about an opportunity with the NFL. This was everybody's dream; to be in the Nation Football League. In the strength conditioning world, if you make it to the NFL it is a big deal. In my opinion, it was even greater than baseball. Not everybody out there would know about strength conditioning, but everybody in the strength conditioning world would say, "Oh, you made it in the NFL; you must be doing something right." Basically, NFL is like a five-star hotel, and MLB is a three or four star.

I was starting to feel a little bit better about myself. But then I would get home tired, late at night, and find myself falling back into those depressed thoughts. There is a definite medical diagnosis of depression, but I don't look at it from diagnosis standpoint anymore. Because what is depression? Again, it goes back to what is truth. I was only making this stuff up in my mind, and I was only claiming that I had depression because I was going to a doctor who told me I was depressed.

You couldn't really see it. There was nothing there. It wasn't something tangible you can see or grab. Did I have irrational thoughts? Yes. I was having irrational thoughts based on the way I was thinking, but not based around depression; not based on something that was tangible. Belief is very powerful and hard to break from the mind. This is unfortunate because if we live our lives with these beliefs, we will forever be a victim. Just consider the world with regards to religion. Thirty-two countries are at war right now. No one on this planet has an absolute truth, and this is a fight as well. A great book to read is the *Biology of Belief* by Bruce Lipton. He really opened me up to the understanding that we only use 5% of our genes. So, life is just perception. We have memories that map out our life. I like to think of us like trees, as a youngster you can bend tip to toe without breaking. As we age, we are left with a tree that will sway, but with the need to love all that we acquired otherwise we will break. So, learning to observe our thoughts allows us to become an impartial witness and consider whether our beliefs are accurate or not Someone may have experienced something unexpected in life that caused a paradigm shift. This is what happened to me. It drove me to seek, and fight a new fight, so I could enjoy my life.

Some antidepressants can cause a side effect of suicidal thoughts. That's the other part of it, which is interesting, too. They tell you that its suicidal thoughts, then you begin to think of suicidal thoughts. So, it's a bunch of bullshit when you finally see what it really is. It just keeps escalating.

Now the fear that you might actually follow through with it starts to become the energy that's self-fulfilling. I think the closest I ever came to it. I never plotted it out, but I had an unbelievable amount of this will to do it. Had my family members not been there; I probably would've done it. That's what I feel. This part of my life was just because I constantly thought about suicide. I wanted to end my life. I wanted to end this overwhelming cycle I was on.

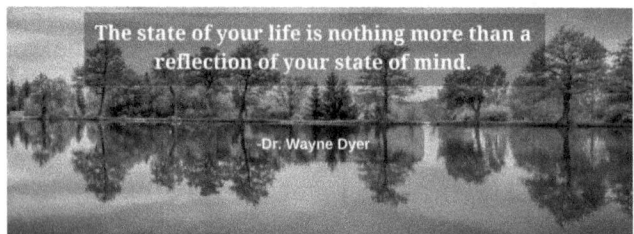

I think it was happening because I was trying to figure out the definition of life. I just got more confused. I think the medication had given me some type of feeling that I hadn't felt before, but it also could've been a placebo effect. So, what I would tell everyone is that you should never let a doctor dictate your life. It's not the medicines that give you the thought. Perhaps it makes it worse; I am not sure. The thoughts are always there. The thoughts were always there, even when I was a kid.

There was a time when someone would joke about it and say, "I wonder what it would be like if I weren't here." And my parents would say, "Don't you ever think like that." So, the thoughts are just regurgitated thoughts. There are no new thoughts in our mind. They're just exacerbated by the understanding that depression exists. But, when I was thinking like that all the time, it became self-fulfilling and an example of the law of attraction.

Realistically, I have gone through it. I would say all of it is bullshit because I came out of it knowing that. But in the mix of things, it was as real as it gets. It's something that, unless you become aware of it, will take over your life. It's happening to people every day because we have these thoughts, concepts and incorrect understandings in our head.

I went to a conference recently. They stated there that in the mental health field itself, they are short 5,000 doctors of psychiatry. Therefore, the general practitioner can distribute these medicines that are normally distributed by psychiatrists. Even this psychologist that I saw was now allowed to do it. She said, "Oh, yeah. I remember being depressed with anxiety and I went on Prozac. It's something you might want to consider." So now you're getting mixed signals. All she was trying to do was help me, but it was helping me in the wrong way. When life is spiritually driven from your inner self, you can accomplish what you want to accomplish.

So, I went through a time when I wasn't open to life. I was at the mercy of the symptoms and diagnosis and began to turn to the diagnosis as a self-fulfilling prophecy.

The same thing applies to what you see in our society of any type of religious-based or belief system that has become an external environment we become accustomed to. You look at ISIS and ask them why they're doing it; they'd say, "I'm doing it because of my belief system." So, a belief is bull. Then you're exasperated by whatever your environment is trying to instill in you. So, it's like there is no real belief in life and that's what this is all leading up to.

That's what I want people to understand. I didn't know who I was, until now. I can speak about it. It sounds philosophical, but its stuff that I have experienced from within a meditated state. It sees the truth. As the saying goes, "You can't see the forest while in the woods." At the time I didn't, because I was asleep to who I really was.

At this stage in my life, I worked part time at the clinic. In the evenings, I would drive over, and I had to be at the Tampa Bay Bucs facility. I'd work in the morning at around 5:30 A.M. and in the evening; I'd try to build up my clientele from 7:00 P.M. or so, until 10:00 P.M. at night. Then I'd finally drive home.

At times, I would drive home and have weird stuff happen with my thoughts. I think I had one of my biggest urges happen to me one night after I went home. I just felt all tingly and like I wanted to leave my body. It was an awfully weird feeling. The urge to end my life had become even stronger. I constantly filled my mind with all these thoughts. The minute something would happen, I would have that thought. It was a scary time.

Even the happiest guy, who I thought was brilliant, suffered from these thoughts, Robin Williams. He changed so many people's lives. Obviously, there were things in his mind that he wasn't aware of or couldn't escape.

The great thing for me was that I was now working at a hospital clinic for personal training and physical therapy. It was going well. I met a lot of cool people, a lot of folks that I helped. The Tampa Bay Bucs were not doing well; I hated that it was such a short stint in the NFL. I was working full-time with them, but it was a part-time gig because it was just a season. I didn't get full-time with them because the head coach had been fired and that was it; that was the end of my career in the NFL.

I was with them for one year; it was a lot of fun. I made it through the whole season with them, but because it was the NFL, in the egotistical mindset of strength conditioning, it felt like I had made it. It also helped with my depression because it was a mood and confidence elevator. It helped me out. In fact, there was a player who helped me out greatly. When I started coming out of depression and started feeling better, it was a football player who had mentioned to me the power of positive thinking.

Football is an interesting beast. They had guys that would make League minimum, which was $430,000 a year. You got paid for six months out of that. Then there was a practice squad. Fifty-three guys were on League minimum and on the practice squad we had six guys. On the practice squad, they weren't making very much money at all. They do just as much work, if not more, to be on that team and there are no guarantees in football. In baseball, if I sign a contract with a baseball team for $175 million, that's what I'd get. Hurt or playing; the player would get $175 million. If a player gets hurt in the NFL, they will not get any of it.

There was a fellow that was always smiling, wearing his headphones, always working, and he never questioned anything. Again, with the Law of Attraction, these people show up in your life. This guy showed up in my life at the perfect time because he came in and I happened to be training them on that day. I said, "Can I ask you a question? Why are you always smiling? You get your ass kicked on the field daily. Some of these guys are making millions of dollars, and they come in pissed off, why are you smiling?" He replied, "I had a lot of help from my dad." So of course, that peaked my interest, so I said "Really? What's your dad doing?" He told me "He's a psychiatrist." I said, "Okay. Give me something positive to read, man. I need some help." He said, "Yeah, a good book to read is *Power of Positive Thinking*." I asked for the author and information for the books, and then I found them.

I got the book, and I couldn't put it down. It was like my mind was finally coming out of a cloud. It was my 'aha moment.' I was intrigued by everything in the book like it was a completely different way of thinking. There's a section in there called '*My True Coming Out*.' I had stopped taking the antidepressants at this point. I still had the Xanax because that occasionally helped me if I needed it.

In fact, I was so paranoid about ensuring I had Xanax on me that I put some in a tiny container and carried it on my keychain. I would go everywhere with that thing, and I felt secure if I had them. That was one thing that made me feel good. So, there I was, I downloaded this book *Power of Positive Thinking*, and I'm still reading it. There was a section in there; it says "Imagine, when you take a shower that the water is filling your mind up and eliminating all the negative thoughts in your head." I started doing that almost every night. Every time I got into the shower, I would do it. I still do it from time to time. I'd take my fingers, and I'd plug up my ears. The impact of the water hitting your skull; you can hear it. My back was to the water. I would walk very slowly, and I would think about all my negative thoughts.

It would be like you put out a bowl and filled it with those thoughts, like when you're washing a bowl in the sink, and you see it, and the suds roll over the top side of it, I envisioned that. I envisioned my thoughts being inside the suds. The minute the water gets to the top of your skull, the water just kind of flows on the top of your face. It felt like I was eliminating and getting rid of all my negative thoughts. I would do that over and over and over again.

One night I just broke down and cried in the shower. That was a release of a lot of what had built up in my mind. Then I would close my mind off. After I dumped all the negative thoughts, I would act the other way. I would face the other way, and I would pretend I was filling my mind up with love, kindness, happiness and all good stuff. That was kind of like my turning point when I started to feel a little better.

I started to train a military lady, at the gym in the hospital wellness center. She was a pretty high ranking officer. She asked me to meet her on base and train there instead because of her busy schedule. So, I started training her at the base in Tampa.

One night after training she noticed, "You know what, you look like you're holding on to some stuff. I can see it in your eyes. You're filled up with all kinds of stuff. Is everything alright?" I cried right there in front of her. I asked, "How do you know that?" She replied, "Because I've dealt with some stuff myself. Are you okay?" I said,

"I've been dealing with anxiety and depression, and I'm working my way through it, but thanks for asking." I kind of left it at that because I didn't really want to disclose anything. So, she asked, "Have you ever heard of Lucinda Bassett?" I said, "Yes, my mother gave me her book. I read it. It's a very good book." She then asked, "Have you done her CDs?" I had not. She said, "They normally give out these CDs to military folks coming back who are suffering from PTSD. It would be good for you to get hold of one. If I can find one in storage, I'll bring it to you." She couldn't find them after a while, so eventually just bought them because I was really intrigued.

They cost about $100. I went through the entire program. There are 15 CDs, a workbook, and other items. I worked through the whole process beginning to end. One of the CDs in there even mentioned Wayne Dyer. Lucinda always had a group session at the end of the CDs, and within the session, there were people just like you and me, talking about their problems. I felt like I wasn't alone.

I could start to see that this depression was not actually real and that they were just irrational thoughts. Lucinda talked about one of her fears that she would stab her husband. That's what anxiety and all that stuff does to you. It gives you irrational thoughts. Eventually, she mentions Wayne Dyer. I rewound it, and I kept writing it down, so I could get his name.

I typed in Wayne Dyer in iTunes, and the first book that popped up was *Wishes Fulfilled*. I didn't even hesitate. I just bought it. Like I said, synchronicity, I'm starting to see more of it. I didn't know what synchronicity was. You see these things pop up. First I found the *Power of Positive*

Thinking book. Then my client sees tears in my eyes one night. Then all of a sudden, all these people are surrounding me with help. I then received more and more of this self-help. After reading Dyer, I no longer was thinking negative thoughts. I was thinking of the positive things in my life. As I thought about the positive things, people showed up, like Marshall, and they'd say to me, "Hey, can you fix me?"

Wayne Dyer's book, *Wishes Fulfilled*, had a sentence or two in there that brought me to tears again because it introduced a new way of thinking. It was the "god" within you. That's what Wayne Dyer talks about. He says that we're all gods with this insane empowerment and that we're all the same. I kept thinking "what does that mean?" Coming from a Catholic background, I didn't understand. I was very confused at what he was trying to say, but it touched me in a way that is hard to express.

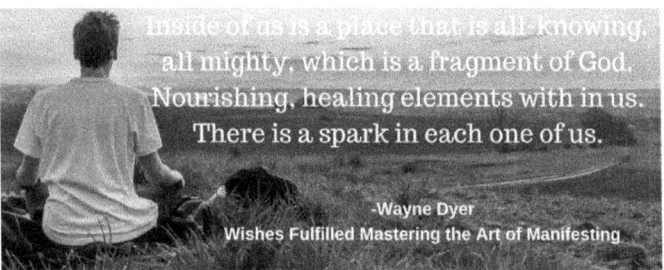

Inside of us is a place that is all-knowing, all mighty, which is a fragment of God. Nourishing, healing elements with in us. There is a spark in each one of us.

-Wayne Dyer
Wishes Fulfilled Mastering the Art of Manifesting

You can't explain it until you go through that experience. I was listening to this material, and I cried a little bit. Denise at this stage was pregnant with our second child. She was there and said, "What's wrong?" and I replied, "I fear that I'm going to lose you. I'm going to lose Lilliana, our first born, and now also with the new baby coming in." And she questioned, "Why is that?" I whispered, "Because I like what Wayne Dyer is saying and I don't know if you'll identify with this transformation in me."

When I met Denise, she wasn't raised a Catholic. Growing up she had often attended Catholic Church on her own. She didn't really have a religion that she was part of. When we got married, there were various sacraments. One of the sacraments of marriage was that you had to first go through communion to be confirmed. I went through all that with her. So, at this stage of my life, she was confused thinking, "Now you're going against the Catholic religion? I don't understand where you're at, but I support you." It was a relief that she supported me and she doesn't see anything wrong with me. I was so scared that she wouldn't understand. So, I let her read the words of Wayne Dyer and his philosophies that surround the concept: *You are the same as your Source. You are God. Because you come from God, you cannot be anything but God.* (http://www.drwaynedyer.com/press/you-are-god-in-depth-conversation-with-dr-wayne-dyer/)

This way of thinking really started my enlightenment and made my thoughts more positive. I experienced Lucinda's work, so I was already getting better. I had gone through the *Power of Positive Thinking*. I had a breakthrough with that. So, at this point in my life, I saw a turnabout for the better.

That being said, I still had tough times and the occasional relapse. Then I advanced onto other folks that Wayne Dyer would mention. I started coming out of that darkness. I was starting to come alive.

Baby number two arrived, and we named her Daniella.

Financially, we were establishing ourselves again after the loss of the baseball job. Still, it was a tough time. When I was let go from the Bucs, I felt horrible. Then I thought, 'you know I had enough of this crap.' I'm glad that I kept the job at the Clinic. I worked there full-time and I worked my ass off.

As I was working through all of this, I was coming out of a funk, too, so I was starting to cheer up. I didn't see it as a hard time as in the past. I realized it was just another challenge put in front of me. I was building up clients, talking to people, general everyday folks. You get friendly with people, and then you see how the world is big, but you're not alone, everyone is just alike.

I started to see by the end of the CD's, that there were more people that I could think of, who were everyday Joes and Jane's, that felt the same way I did. So, what was I worried about?

This is when I finally started growing into my true self. I started to see positive affirmations, and I listened to all the stuff that was coming to me. It was all relative to that enlightenment; coming out because this was who I truly was. I met the right people at the right time. One of my mentors, whom I met at the hospital, had a bad back for 25 years. I fixed his back, and he loved me. He said, "you know, you're too talented." I am very grateful to this guy, Marshall. He changed my career path completely. He changed my way of thinking. The positivity was pouring in at this point. People were saying, "Oh, you've got to see Luke, he's the man." He said, "I've seen orthos, I've seen chiropractors, I've seen acupuncturists. I've seen all these people, and in twenty-five years nobody has ever done what you've done to fix me." He was very grateful and still is, and I'm grateful for him because he's in my life.

Marshall told me that I should open my own business.
He told me that I could make a lot more money training under my own single versus the wellness center taking their cuts. He motivated me about my skills and kept telling me I could do it on my own.

I started to get back on my feet and was excited about business opportunities again. I was listening to all of Wayne Dyer's audio books. I'd take Cujo out for a walk and sit down on a bench and just listen to stories. Synchronicity was all around me now. Positive people kept showing up in my life, one after another after another. It kept coming, more positive and more encouraging, and things have just blown up from there. The beginning of a wonderful life.

"Seeing your own life more clearly involves being acutely aware of anything and everything that creates excitement within your being. If it excites you, the very presence of that inner excitement is all the evidence you need to remind you that you're aligned with your true essence. When you are following your bliss, you are most amenable to receiving guidance from the spiritual realm. This is called synchronicity—a state in which you almost feel as if you are in a collaborative arrangement with fate."

~Wayne Dyer's interpretation of synchronicity from his blog: http://www.drwaynedyer.com/blog/the-real-message-in-memoir/

Chapter 10: MOBILITY RX

So, Marshall had started to discuss some of the numbers of starting my own business. He described it in a much easier way for me to understand how I could make more money than just working for the wellness center. I started to get excited again. I was a little nervous because of the first gym that didn't work out so well in Mike's facility. So, I had some reservations when I told Denise I think I wanted to open my own business. She asked, "Do you have a business plan?" and I answered, "Not really." I figured I could just make it work.

Most of my clients were localized in one area. So, I went up the owner of a gym in that region, and I asked, "I'm looking for a place, a little shack where I can set up shop. I don't want anything big. I just want to put a table in there, and I want to work with some people and occasionally use some of your equipment, but you can charge me whatever you need to charge me if it's fair." He retorted, "No I'm not interested." So, I understood, "No problem."

I kept looking around, and there was a sign right next to his place in the strip mall. I contacted the owner to find out how much it was to rent, and she replied: "$1,100.00" and she agreed to meet me up there. It was July, and it was raining. When she came in, she had her contract with her just in case. She showed me the place, and I started visualizing what I could do with it. It was a single unit, about maybe 900 square feet. I began to think this looked like it might work. I guess I didn't know what I was getting into. I didn't know any of the clauses in the contract. I thought it was a residential thing, so I just signed away. I thought, 'Let's do it. I can afford it. I can figure it out.' I had all the wind behind me. So, I signed the papers and I opened up my shop.

Denise was working at TICO, I phoned her and exclaimed, "Hey, you're talking to the new owner of a workout facility in Clearwater!" I was so excited goosebumps were tingling up and down my arms. I couldn't wait to share the news with her. She quickly responded, "Oh, that's cool. I have to go back to work."

When I got home, I was not sure how Denise was feeling about this decision I made. . She was not at all happy that I jumped into the business without a plan. I had thought she might have been thrilled with me, but she was upset. As we were lying in bed I felt the need to ask over and over are you mad at my decision to start the business. Denise's "it's too late go out and sell" Our second daughter had just been born. We had a lot of bills and responsibilities. However, since I'd already signed the contract, all I could do was just to go ahead and do it. I fell right to sleep once I had Denise's thoughts.

Some time ago in my career, I worked for an electric company, and I learned how to do electrical work. I saw people building in the carpentry end and learned how to frame. So, I kind of taught myself how to do a lot of that stuff and that's not necessarily the way to go; because inspectors come in and check all of that. But being new to this again, I didn't know, so I just started tearing walls down and doing what I needed to do. I made it work. I ended up buying some used gym equipment off Craig's List. And I bought some new equipment, and I found this and that, and I put it all together, and I had a business going. I was pretty scared at first. The name of my business is Mobility RX, and that name came about because I was seeing clients on the truck and I wanted to have a local name that was going to be recognized eventually as a branded name. Through this Mobility RX, I wanted to build and represent myself. It's not like PT on wheels. I wanted to have a recognizable name, so 'Mobility' was my first choice. This was because I was mobile when we started and I was bringing mobility back to the people that I was seeing.

It's interesting, but ever since I could recall, I think blue has been one of my favorite colors. I had an old blue jeep, followed by this blue Tacoma. So, everything representing this mobility is blue. Then one day a client of mine that I was training over here in St. Pete was wearing some Adidas shoes that had neon green at the top. I looked down thought 'what interesting colors.' As Wayne Dyer said, things show up, when you're looking for something. I was looking for a logo with the right colors and this combination of appeared.

I decided that I should create my own business plan. There was no time like the present. That was my start of it, and it was the best start ever. People were coming to me, and I didn't even have proper flooring yet. I had this flooring that was concrete that I had painted with a specific paint that was meant for a garage. I did the best I could do, with the money that I had starting up. I put it all on my credit card. So, that's how I got started, and now it's a flourishing business. It's going well; it's rolling, and I'm going into my fourth year.

All my business was coming to fruition. I wanted to expand, and many people suggested, "Just hire another person." But, I couldn't figure out how I could do that without it costing a hundred grand. I didn't want to hire just a trainer to come in and then have to train them. I wanted whoever came in, to do things 'Luke's way'.

I believe the business has come about, by the Law of Attraction. Any mistakes I've made, I've learned from, and I consider them all positive mistakes. There's nothing negative in my life, although back then I saw them as negative.

I learned a lot what gym equipment was good and bad, and I knew what equipment my competitors had. I had TVs and iPods etc., and am thinking about expansion.

Things are growing and going well, and I'm working on more people. There are more referrals, and more people are coming because of painful backs and shoulders. I'm grateful and thankful. That's why I want people to read this and gain the impression that it's not all about truth. Because if I was not open to see that these things could happen, I would've been stuck in my ways and still doing a nine to five job, and I'd be miserable.

One of Wayne Dyer's key messages was to send everybody love. I look back at everything in my life and know that it happened for a reason, at the right time. I was exactly where I was meant to be in my life. Now, I can look back at everything in retrospect. If it weren't for baseball, I wouldn't have had the knowledge to fix these people. If it weren't for the Busy Body job, I wouldn't have the knowledge about what gym equipment to buy. If I didn't work at my first fitness place, I wouldn't have known about business in the first place. If I didn't have anyone of these experiences, I would have been too scared even to make the attempt to start a business.

There's a quote, which says something along the lines of: 'you can't see the forest when you're in the woods.' That's an important quote for me because I wouldn't have seen any of what I experienced if I just listened to everybody and continued down the path of what somebody else wanted for me.

So, that's been a big help for me to be willing to change. But, the change came from something that was very, very scary. It was a panic attack, and that felt so real. That shook my entire foundation of what I thought my life was. I'm grateful for the fact that my body went through that shock. Greatness comes from deep pain. Sometimes we must experience that pain in order to become aligned with our true self. To find our way of our highest calling.

With my experience in baseball, I learned how to be a father because I had to deal with 25 guys all the time. I learned how to cope with different attitudes and different people. I did it via the old Luke way of thinking; contemplating how I'd whip their ass. At the time I was resentful, angry, and I wanted them to do things my way. I learned, however, that not everybody was going to do it my way. Now that I have kids I have realized they're not going to do it my way either. So, as they say, you should 'pick your battles wisely.' It's such a wonderful experience to have kids. The moment I first realized I was becoming a father I was scared, but I then realized, I was already a father. I didn't know baseball was my warm up practice.

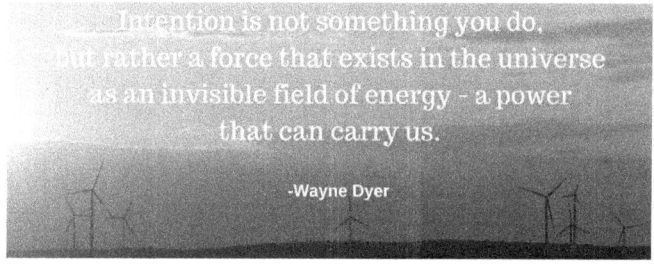

Intention is not something you do, but rather a force that exists in the universe as an invisible field of energy - a power that can carry us.

-Wayne Dyer

Chapter 11: INVENTION

I have an invention that I have a 12-page patent on. For now, I call it: 'Luke's Arm' because it represents my arm and what I do. 95 percent of all back injuries are fused at the O5S1, which is your sacral joint. On a daily basis, most people who spend time sitting will have some type of pelvic tilt; it tends to shift the pelvis or the ileum away from the sacral joint. It's known as a sacroiliac joint, and so that becomes loosened by the ligaments and becomes worn out from the daily grind. When that takes place, then this shift, or this inferior pull, is based around a couple of things: one is either how the person sleeps or sits, or possibly a structural imbalance due to femur and leg length. It's common with many people. I saw one lady in Disney walking, probably the worst case I've ever seen. She had a fully functioning leg, but her foot was at the middle part of her thigh, and then the rest went all the way down. She had a knee and was able to bend it fine. But she had a metal rod that went down to her shoe—a prosthetic leg. So, she probably was as straight as an arrow, but she had to lug around a titanium leg, so it caused her some physical issues. As far as the discrepancy with legs, it simply takes a millimeter to be off and cause someone major physical complications. I have some patients that are six to 10 millimeters off, so they must use little lifts for their shoes. It's more common than most people would think, but it causes sciatica syndrome; though not true sciatica. True sciatica is a muscular imbalance, but sciatica syndrome may develop if your hip is in a bad place. This will give you the feelings of sciatica, which is still unpleasant. You're still going to get numbness. You're still going to get the burning and tingle ease and all the symptoms that go with sciatica. But what my 'Luke's Arm' device does, is to manipulate that joint back into place, but not from being from a chiropractic manipulation, it's doing it with muscle activation. So, you would manipulate your pelvis back into a position by using this device.

You lie down on your back flat; bring your knees up, so your feet are flat. This device will Velcro onto your legs, and then you hold like a metal rod in between them to give you more stability. Then you push and pull, and when you push and pull, you're pushing one pelvis up and one pelvis down; then you push and pull the opposite way. I call it Luke's Arm because if I was manipulating someone, I'd put my arm up underneath and cup it on one side, and the person would have their arm underneath. They'd push against my forearm, and it would shift their hip one way, and then I'd go the other side, and they shift their hip the other. I'd then place my forearm and hand in between their legs, and then they'd squeeze, and when they do this, it causes their hips to flare out. I then get them to push out; they adduct both ways. This means the pelvis would naturally go back to where it was supposed to be. Sometimes you'll feel a little click or pop when your pelvis does this. That's your SI joint, and/or it could be pubic since it's going back into place as well; they call it a shotgun adjustment. I learned this adjustment in baseball because guys would come in with bad backs. And one of the guys I worked with, Jose, showed us all how to do this. He said it was useful, and that if you've ever had your lower back go out on you, you know the debilitating pain that you can feel. It's just like that crunchy; take your breath away feeling. I was doing this adjustment and people were getting better, and I wondered: 'how can I help more people?' So, I came up with the invention of Luke's Arm.

This will be able to help people who aren't able to stay local. I've got one guy that flew down from Philadelphia, and I fixed his back while he was here. He stayed here four weeks, but I'm making one now currently for him, because he said that he went from an eight or nine, down to a one or two pain wise. He wants Luke's magic touch to get him back and to keep him at a one or a two; because the pain might have traveled back up to a three or four.

Because he's been doing the exercise, He's been holding steady. But he still has those days where, he wants to stay at a two, and not increase to a three or four, or get rid of the pain completely. So, the maintenance that he was doing with me I'd have him do it with my device, and he was continuing to improve. I mean, in four weeks we changed this guy's life. So, he went from being a medical doctor who could no longer work, due to not being able to move, to now being at a stage where he can move a little bit. So, my device does work. It also worked on Marshall to cure him of twenty-five years of back pain.

I tell everybody to not have back surgery; I ask them to let me work on them. I just received another review two days ago, from a physician. She gave me a great review. She's been a medical doctor, with 20 years in her field, and her physical condition has improved. She had epidurals and all kinds of treatment, prior to coming to me. She was scared to come, but she made her way up to my facility. She was very open to seeing what I could do. It follows the theme of truth.

I can definitely fix anybody's back. There are always other alternatives to traditional medicine. There are people like me all around the world, which are offering these alternatives. I want everyone to know the secret techniques I have. I'm able to perform it on people. I want my methods out in the open; it's possible that someone may come up with a better idea. Maybe they can come up with something creative. There are so many creative people out there that they can take a twist on yours, and implement, and then have their own business. They may flourish. But you still flourish because they still need you. Your factory will keep rolling.

I have a burning desire-an inner flame that will not be extinguished by outer forces-to know and live from higher regions, to be transformed so that my new concept of myself will no longer include any limitations. I am willing to challenge and change any thoughts that impede my having a higher vision of myself.

-Wayne Dyer
Wishes Fulfilled: Mastering the Art of Manifesting

CHAPTER 12: I AM

We were getting ready to go to church one morning, and I kept my Xanax in my pocket. I would take it out at night and put them on my dresser. At this point I rarely took them, but I *had* to have them with me. Denise hopped in the car, and I backed up not even thinking about it, and then I remembered, "Oh crap, I forgot my Xanax." We were already down the road from our house at this point. Denise said, "Don't worry about it, you'll be fine. By the time you take it anyway, it's already past. So why are you so worried about it?" I said, "I got to have it." She responded, "No if you turn around, we're going to be late. Just go, you'll be fine."

I went to church and had to sweat it out. I was in rough shape because I was aware that I left it at home and was freaking out on the way there. Sitting in church and that's all I could think about. When I made it through, it became a huge confidence builder. I realized I didn't need to have that the Xanax. That's not a part of my life anymore; I could let it go.

I've always had a really strong will. That's the spirit I see when I reflect on all of this. When I talk about that feeling I would get in my belly when I was 16, I think it's in all of us. For example, my father challenged me one time in high school. He said, "I bet you can't quit drinking your soda products." He bet me $20 saying I had to quit for a month. So, I didn't drink soda for a month, and I won the bet. I have not had *any* more soda since. Pure will!

What I'm saying is that once it's there, I'm pretty good with it. Once I gave up with Xanax, I was done. These are the commitments that I know today that I try to share with people. When you make a full commitment to something, you can change your life completely. There's a lot of research done on this stuff with epigenetics and everything that takes place in life. Epigenetics is defined as the study of changes in organisms caused by modification of gene expression rather than alteration of the genetic code itself. I beat drinking soda. I changed my desire for it in within my own body. The only thing that I drink now is water. I used to drink sweet tea, and then I went to unsweet tea, little by little until I eventually beat it.

When the time came to get rid of the Xanax, Denise said, "You don't need it," and I saw that I could beat it, I realized that I was stronger. Then there was the voice that was telling me that I needed to have it, there's a mental thought that's traveling with all of us that tempts us. Every day, they're just recycled thoughts. That's all they are.

They're not your true thoughts until you put it into action. Then it becomes your real existence, or what you perceive to be real. It's like if a thought is there, that's okay, that's just a memory of what the brain remembers. The existence of what we are; there's more to that. There's more to who you are than this existence of somebody else's explanation. We've talked about that in previous chapters, of trying to find your own identity.

After I started reading all these books, I finally went away from the Catholic Church. I chose this not to denounce it, but I have been trying to transcend ever since I've learned about this other knowledge. I've been trying to have in the words of Wayne Dyer True Nobility; *It's about being better than I once was.* That's the part of my life I've transcended, the Catholicism belief system. I'm not saying there weren't good times and things that came from Catholicism. It probably kept me grounded at times when I was bowing, but I think that there's a lot of Catholicism that I disagree with at the present moment. It sounds ridiculous, to think that I even believed in the religion at times, like heaven, hell, purgatory or being condemned for even lusting over other women.

I think it is absurd when someone attempts to tell me what's taking place in my life. If I am in charge of this body, how can somebody else control it? I saw it first and foremost with the antidepressants, the drugs, and the doctors. They were telling me all this stuff, and it didn't work. It only lessened my anxiety for the moment; the doctors might have then said, "Oh you've got to take another drug. Or you're symptomatically treating it." I didn't ever get any better.

Life again is about experiences. If you have an experience with a drug, and it didn't work for you; it may work for somebody else. I'm not saying for everybody to do what I did to feel better, but I'm saying that there is hope and that there are other options besides a psychiatrist, a psychologist, a general practitioner or medication. There are more options available to get to where you want to be. If you want to stay in that environment and you're okay just taking the Xanax, then there's nothing wrong with that. I'm not saying it's wrong for anybody, just that there are other options.

Throughout this process, I have learned that meditation helps and it has become a huge part of my life. Initially, I didn't really know what it was all about; only what somebody told me it was. You have to figure out what it is for you. Some people call it prayer, some call it meditation. Either way you look at it, you're saying something that is in your mind, connotatively measured that is helpful or not helpful. Like I told you, the biggest thing in depression was that I was telling myself over and over, that these are the thoughts that were taking place in my mind.

We can analyze this all day long and dissect it. We can sit there and apply medical terms all day long, but those are just terms. Nobody knows how birth starts, or how death starts, or ends, or whatever actually takes place. We just have concepts and ideas that have been fed to us. There are all these questions. So, when you think about all your prayers, or about self-fulfilling prophecies, you're still putting that into practice no matter which way you look at it or how you describe that.

When I go into meditation every day, I do so for about 45 minutes to an hour. From Wayne Dyer's perspective, he would say the most powerful thing in the world is the, "I am discourse." The "I am" is from an old scripture from Moses, where Moses was met with a burning bush, and he said, "What am I?" Moses was told that "I am that I am." So, when you break that down, as I understand it, the most important thing to Wayne Dyer is *I am*. If you put the, *I am* in everything that means you're describing who you are by anything that you see. You do this when you look at a tree and say, I am that, and when you look at your desk and say, I am that. Now the reason why you're saying this is because you are the god within you. This can be a little confusing for some people. To better understand, look at yourself and close your eyes for a moment. You can see something that you love, or you want, or something in your life that you can get a full description of. If you close your eyes and you think of your mother, and you say I want to picture my mom, you can get a clear image of her within minutes. If you close your eyes and you think of a sunset, you can get a clear image of a sunset. So anytime you do this process, where is that taking place? Because if you open your eyes back up, the images aren't there.

So, when Wayne Dyer was stating this, he said the most important thing in life is *I am* before any statements. What he's stating is that it's only happening within you. Science tells us the same thing from an atom standpoint. When you break an atom down to subatomic matter and look at quantum physics under a microscope, you see that we don't even exist. That's what science tells us: that we're 99% not even here. That's because we block the sun, or we block the light that's reflecting on us, that's the reason we get an image.

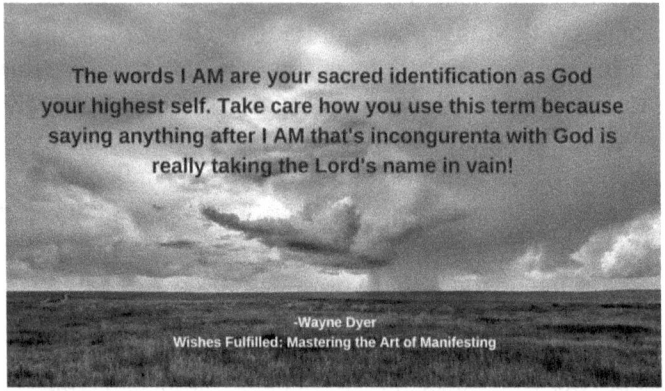

The words I AM are your sacred identification as God your highest self. Take care how you use this term because saying anything after I AM that's incongurenta with God is really taking the Lord's name in vain!

-Wayne Dyer
Wishes Fulfilled: Mastering the Art of Manifesting

There's such a thing as collective conscious energy. If, for example, there's something on television that people focus all their energy on; they can record the conscious levels, and it'll shoot back. That's what I think Wayne Dyer means when he talks about how we're all one god and that the universe is the one source of what we are. It's just that we're broken up into this flesh so that we can experience things through our physical body.

There's a man who works out with me, and he told me that when he was at UCF, he wrote an article in his philosophy class. It was based on the fact that there can't be a God and free will at the same time. And so, I asked, "Do you ever believe that you are a god?" He said, "No." I asked, "Why not?" He said, "Because that's all omnipresent, you know." I replied, "Yeah, but that's just a thought." The thought that is a man-made definition of what a god might be. I said, "Why do you negate yourself?"

Later, he asked, "But what about lions? You know when they have an argument about what they're eating, and they try to fight each other."

I replied, "Well, they don't have the intellect as a human being. You can't associate a lion with a human being. They're in their own world, so the five senses kick in, and they're just expressing themselves based around trying to survive, just trying to eat." I said, "But we have the intellect, and we know how to eat, and we know how to do what we need to do. Play with other folks, other souls."

And then he contemplated, "Well, what about ants? Or do you think they're just as powerful?"

I said, "Sure. Did you ever see an ant?" I said, "That damn thing carries like four times his body weight all around; if we had a damn car that was made like an ant, we would be indestructible, you know."

I advised him to start looking at the flesh of things and then separate it into the soul. The soul can do anything it wants to do, but because we're in the flesh, we are limited. He said, "Then we're not gods." I replied, "No." I said, "We are gods."

He asked why I was separating this, and I replied, "Because...how can you express yourself if you don't have the flesh? You can't express yourself. You can only live your life in the other realm. I mean we're already doing that. We're in the world of expressing ourselves through human contact."

When people complain and moan about their current situation, I want to point out, that they chose to be a certain race, a certain ethnicity, and certain poverty level. They chose that life and those challenges. Everyone should get to choose what challenges they want to experience within this lifetime. These are not setbacks; these are lessons. I know many people will not see it that way. That they were dealt a bad hand in life. But these are just obstacles that once you conquer will unravel the best existence you have ever wished for.

Wayne Dyer's "I am," is where I started. Then I thought more deeply on this; Deepak Chopra talks about it from the medical side, as well as the spiritual side. *Deepak Chopra is an American author, public speaker, alternative medicine advocate, and a prominent figure in the New Age movement. Through his books and videos, he has become one of the best-known and wealthiest figures in alternative medicine* ~ Wikipedia.

Chopra talks about a guide. Mind you, I have been seeking this for six years, and it just happened. Chopra talked about the acronym SIFT (SENSATIONS, IMAGES, FEELINGS AND THOUGHTS) and so the *I am discourse* matches this completely by saying that if I see something if I hear something, if I touch something, it's only taking place in your mind, but not on a physical mind.

The physical mind only shows synapses, but really nothing takes place in the mind. So where was it taking place? You can say memory is stored in your mind. Where's the mind that is storing it? It's not there, right? So, if it's stored in your skin, can I take one of those photo books that you used to have when you were a kid? When you put it up to some light, can you see your memory from your skin? You got to take a piece out and say, "Oh there's my fifth grade." Like where is it because I'm not the fifth-grader anymore. I'm going on 37.

When you start to think like that, and you start to meditate or pray, these are the thoughts that come. When you think about them long enough, they show up in your life. If you want something to show up in your life, if you want 1 million dollars to show up in your life, think about it and pray on it. Do it every single day and 1 million dollars will show up in your life. I'm not saying that you have to be a billionaire, or that you have to be a millionaire, or that you have to be the poorest person. What I'm saying is whatever you think about in your life that you want to expand upon, that's what you should meditate and pray on.

Even in fundamental religion, there are a few differences. When I was Catholic, I would write a little sticky note up and hand it to God. I would say, "Take care of my problems." I would only do that once a week. Like 'man, my brother John's being an asshole, help me out.' So, you do that one time and John's still John, his personality didn't change. So, there's a reason why when you pray about it. What's happening is that you're transforming yourself because you're seeing things differently now. John didn't change because I was praying on it every night. Guess what? I helped myself. It's simple when you think about it like that. There doesn't have to be this overly thoughtful process that you have to do.

You can go out there and you can find anything on Google; just type it in, one word, and you got it. But sometimes too much intellectual activity or information clogs our thinking, our wisdom. When we have too much clutter, we start to destroy ourselves, and put ourselves off the path of wisdom.

I heard a story once about this young lady who went to a guru in India and underwent the guru's training. After she was prepared and educated in his wisdom, she was able to use her third eye. Supposedly she can be blindfolded but can still actually read stuff in front of her that people put down in writing. I am not sure where this story came from, but it intrigues me. The interpretation I put on it my own. I think of the three girls that we have now. Denise and I are teaching the youngest about words and putting them together. When I ask her, "Where are your eyes?" She points as if her fingers were. She doesn't know how to speak much yet, but she'll point to my eyes and she'll kind of try to touch them, or my ears, or whatever. So recognition starts at that age and it becomes a memory. That's all we are, as if accumulated from memories of this earth, memories of our present and past, that the richest of people cannot buy back; memories that give us an affinity for that which we all once experienced. Did the girl with the third eye have some kind of extra-sensory perception? Who knows! It's a great story to appropriate for one's own wisdom.

Wayne Dyer told me to do the "I am," so when you think about *I am*, you think about something, and you put *I am* before your thoughts. That was one way he told me how to meditate. Another example Dyer gave was to chant.

You can go out there and you can find anything on Google; just type it in, one word, and you got it. But sometimes too much intellectual activity or information clogs our thinking, our wisdom. When we have too much clutter, we start to destroy ourselves, and put ourselves off the path of wisdom.

I heard a story once about this young lady who went to a guru in India and underwent the guru's training. After she was prepared and educated in his wisdom, she was able to use her third eye. Supposedly she can be blindfolded but can still actually read stuff in front of her that people put down in writing. I am not sure where this story came from, but it intrigues me. The interpretation I put on it my own. I think of the three girls that we have now. Denise and I are teaching the youngest about words and putting them together. When I ask her, "Where are your eyes?"She points as if her fingers were. She doesn't know how to speak much yet, but she'll point to my eyes and she'll kind of try to touch them, or my ears, or whatever. So recognition starts at that age and it becomes a memory. That's all we are, as if accumulated from memories of this earth, memories of our present and past, that the richest of people cannot buy back; memories that give us an affinity for that which we all once experienced. Did the girl with the third eye have some kind of extrasensory perception? Who knows! It's a great story to appropriate for one's own wisdom.

So if I were to teach you that you don't have eyes, that you have a third eye, and you close your eyes and see everything as if you were blind, there is something to that. That's the beauty of the exercise --to find a different path of perception and experience. That's kind of what I'm getting at. It's what you make of it; it's what you want out of meditation. Now, as I noted earlier about my anxiety and depression, I can tell you at this moment that the only thing I obsess about in my life is seeking out more of happiness, more peace and compassion.

I follow an Indian yogi by the name of Sadhguru. I went through his course called *Inner Engineering*. I would recommend it to everyone, once the timing is right for them, when they're ready for it. Wayne Dyer said that the student would seek the teacher when the student is ready. That's very true because if you hear something foreign to you, you'll be turned off by it, and won't let that idea sink in. If you seek it out when you're ready to seek it out, and you're intrigued by it, curious rather than taught about it; it's really a cool experience.

"Sadhguru is a realized yogi, mystic and visionary who has dedicated himself to the elevation of the physical, mental, and spiritual wellbeing of all people."
https://www.innerengineering.com/ieo-new/sadhguru/

The guru that I've mentioned is called Mystique. The reason I mentioned him, was because he has got three million volunteers. It's called the E-ship program. It's a seven-day program, and you meditate on the last day. There I was, sobbing on the last day. I've only ever told four people that that happened to me.

Guru did a blessing, and it was like a release somehow. I'm not sure what happened. The program requires sitting and doing 90 minutes of this. It's not just straight meditation. What he does is he talks for 85 minutes and then the last five or ten minutes might be a short meditation. Then you answer questions before you get to the next day. Every day, I woke up extra early, I'd go to a room, lock the door, and I would sit and listen to the program. That was the only time I could do it. I still get up about 5:00 A.M. every morning. I go out to the pool, and I have a little quiet time to myself. Denise bought me a meditation pillow, and I have chanting beads. I do all kinds of different rituals that I found myself. It keeps me focused in my thoughts, and I'm not in the negative space where I once was.

I used to think that the chanting was going to get me what I needed, but it was not the chanting. It was the Ohms, the actual sound during the chanting. What I learned from the Sadhguru, is that if you cut your tongue out, Ohm would be the only sound you could make. It's very interesting that even from the beginning of time we wouldn't have this vocabulary developed. We would only have this small amount of vibration, like what my third daughter Cassandra does. She doesn't know how to speak, but she knows how to communicate with me.

I do the chanting. I do it all. The funny thing is my neighbors hear it early in the morning. One of them mentioned, "Oh, you do your yoga out there." So, I'm sure they heard it.

My uncle, I told you about, the priest, I talked to him, and he feels liberated when I talk to him because there's not one person out there that has the answer. The Pope talks very highly about stuff that you and I are touching on, but he's still not giving up Catholicism. It's like if you relinquish the Catholicism and you're talking about it, there's probably a little bit more power in that. It's not that Catholicism is bad; I'm not here to condemn and say the Catholicism is bad, nor any religion for that matter. I'm saying that for the girls' sake, and mine, mainly mine. If the girls want to know, I don't want to discourage them.

Everything is just a story, whether it's the stories about Christ or the stories about Buddha. You still have to decide if they're true or not. So, if everything in life is still a story, you have the right to follow it or not to follow it. Even if Christ himself, or Buddha walked into my room and said, "Hey, I'm Christ", we still have to choose, make a choice, even with a hundred miracles happening in front of us. We still have to choose. In our society, we're still driven by a belief system, be it in democracy, faith, patriotism, militarism, environmentalism or whatever demands some kind of response. However, we should be able to say, "wait, let me see your driver's license," your legal permission to engage me, a tag evidencing a license granted. I need a buffer of sorts. We don't have to say, "You're not Christ, let me see some proof." For me, however, I would not mind what any wise or unknown person said to me. I am not a one religion only person. I want to be associated with many because there are so many stories out there based upon a belief system, which I think, from my own perspective, is neat. This idea that nothing or no one religion has gotten it exactly right yet makes lots of sense. There are thirty-two countries at war over beliefs. Figure that. And there are thirty-two different belief groups that haven't yet been able to stop these wars. The value of a belief is the number of things it can or can't explain. Can any belief out there explain why they can't stop war? It is because their belief isn't strong enough? Not sure! So much eternal questioning but no resolution!

So, my point is, if science tells us that everything is made up in our minds. Then, at the end of the day, that's what our souls are telling us too; that we can make a decision. That's what free will is all about. It's awesome because I feel like that's a part of my life. It's the willpower, free will, and all these things coming back to fruition. My power was right here, right now. Because we can't say to ourselves at any point in our lives, it's true or not true. The reason for this is because quantum physics tells us, "Hey, you don't even exist." So, if we don't exist, then it only matters if you let it matter to you. If you see something out there that's pissing you off; it's only because it's in your mind. It didn't really exist according to quantum physics. So, we have the choice to let it affect us or not.

We have the choice to be miserable or happy at any moment of our lives. But in order to do that, we must see ourselves for who we are, not from someone else's perspective, thoughts and beliefs. Because if we're stuck in a paradigm and seeing ourselves at the fingertips of the doctor that says you have depression, or at the fingertips of your family, your President, or whoever, that creates the confusion. You're only going to believe what you think you are. If you want to change at any time, you'd say, "Well that part annoyed me. But if it annoyed me enough, I don't want to live that way anymore."

Even sickness is this way. It's like if you get the flu. Sickness is all based on a memory, that's based around a childhood sickness that you got. Now it's explained to you by mom and dad and said, "Oh that's the flu." Or the doctor says, "Oh that's the flu." But really, what is it? It's just a symptom or a feeling. It could be a cool feeling if we really wanted to be, but we don't. We're making it into a negative one. But it could be connotatively measured at any given point.

It's like people who drink beer and alcohol, and then they throw up. Throwing up doesn't feel awesome, but we do it with alcohol, right? Those are our choices. The flu could feel just as good if we made ourselves believe that it feels good, just as we feel good while we drink.

I just want to continue to summarize this in the sense of from where we first were. To the stage of bringing awareness to people that whatever world we're in, whatever thought we just said, we can change the way we think at any moment, but first, we must *want* to change. I want to go to where people could use my service, and I can give back to people. For those who are unable to pay, I will do charitable work. I can take care of people, and this becomes how I'm presenting myself.

People say that life is nothing more than accumulation, and what you make of that accumulation; even if you are born into a life of poverty, or you're born into a life of wealth. Wherever you're born, it still has to be your thoughts that encompass your life. Because no matter the thoughts, the emotions, and the SIFT (Sensations, Images, Feelings and Thoughts) that's we're talking about, if you're born into poverty, you could still be like Oprah Winfrey! That's a perfect example. She was born into poverty, she was a maid. She's a billionaire today, but only because she changed her SIFT. She changed part of her mentality to reflect what she wanted out of her life. People tend to make paradigms of what has been driven into their mind, based around what poverty is, or based on what wealth is; I did this. It's like where in the Catholic church you have to give ten percent of your wages to the church. I know my parents gave ten percent. That's huge. Ten percent of whatever they made when my mom was a stay-at-home mom. This could be five to ten thousand dollars a year. This was expected of people, but I questioned this, and thought that I should be able to give what I wanted to give, when I wanted to. Giving to the church and the poor, has been instilled in us and we feel guilty or, as in the example of the church, that we'll go to hell if we don't.

All I want is for people to be open enough to allow themselves to become who they want to be rather than what they are told to be.

It doesn't matter what you're doing because, at the end of the day, you know what truth is. Nobody knows if we exist, or if we don't exist. Because the person that's telling you that you exist, does he exist? That's what quantum physics is saying. It's a confusing thing; we can be 95 and still going over this, but then we've wasted our whole life.

So, experience what you want to, and don't do it from someone else's experience. Bite into the apple, bite into whatever you want in life, and figure out what's good for you. If it fits you, then go for it. At the end of the day, it doesn't matter unless it matters to you. That's how I see it, and that's what my message is about. Find something that changes you and helps you. But I just think that there's so much a person can achieve. There's not one thing that is more powerful than the other. There's not one cancer story that's more powerful than another. Nor is one depression or anxiety story more powerful than a cancer story.

We're all in this together, and I think that whatever you want to make out of your life, you'll do so you're willing. That's the cool thing about it. The more you question, the more you'll figure out what you want.

I want people to question everything. I want people to look within themselves and try to get to know themselves. To ask themselves questions such as: Are you feeling happy? Are you feeling miserable? I want people to be aware, open-minded and awake.

Wayne Dyer talks about EGO, meaning Edging God Out of your life. I think that's powerful for me. It's important to bring that back to life for people and never to forget that we're in this battle with ego versus our true self. I said to someone, "Man, I think doctors have it incorrect." I said, "I think we're all bipolar. It's just how we handle it.

So many times, we label each other based on a certain belief, and that's nothing more than an egotistical mindset. People have god within them. The Bible has been translated 3000 times, and I've read it; it's great. But one of the things in there is the minute you label something, you negate it because you put it in a box.

I'm not sure about creation. I think that there's some type of Creator and that maybe the Creator is nothing more than all of us that put it together in manifest form. I would love to inspire people to look through some of the sources that I've read: Wayne Dyer's book, or Deepak Chopra' stuff. I want people to find their own truth.

I don't want people to read mine and say Luke's right. Read this and then go find your own way. To people like

Denise, who said, "you just sound like a normal Joe. Why are you even writing your book?" My experiences may not sound that bad because you didn't live them, but for me, they bruised me, like in a fight.

In my earlier life, I was already trapped by ego. That was the problem because I'd swallowed beliefs, which are very powerful. Beliefs are hard to break.

I told my mom that there's something more that I'm seeking than just a mere staple or happiness. There's a drive, and it brings me to tears, but I don't want to push this onto anyone. I want people to live their life.

The more I find myself questioning, the more I get my answers. The more I get my answers, the easier my life becomes. That's really what it's all about, just trying to question everything. People who are looking for a result, the ones that are looking for help, that's really what I have a desire to support. It's what my heart pours out to be because I know that I went through a lot in my own life.

With people, it's fine if you don't like the way they're doing things. By preventing it, it's the equivalent of taking that other person's toy away, like children in a sandbox.

All through our early childhood, we do things instinctively; then we start following Mom and Dad and then following the pack. Everything is done for children, and their empire is built up around them, which becomes the ego.

I would like a million people to read this book. But, however many people read the book, if it makes people wonder, think, change their mind and makes a better place for them, I'll be pleased. People are stuck in paradigms. Questioning the truth is essential. If someone is doing something that's harmful to you, then you must step back, see that, and question. Ask why are they doing it? Is it harming you because you don't like it based on a belief, based on a definition? Or is it harming you physically? If it's harming you physically, then we all need to step in and figure it out. If it's just mentally, which most is, then it really doesn't matter.

If I can do my own little part, in my own world and people want to be part of that, then life is good. I think we're here just to change the minds of the people that want to be changed or that might be on that same field of perception.

Finding truth is important. You can question existence. You can question religion. You can question all the big fundamentals that are in our lives. Question them and don't be ashamed because nobody has the answers.

In my younger years, I felt fear. One of my biggest fears was a fear of death. Question everything, and then even question death. When you question it, then you can see that the definitions of death are nothing really to fear. It's just a definition because no-one has experienced it. I, myself, have no desire to just yet.

I feel relief that I'm able to let go of the thoughts that just kept me trapped, scared, and fearful. Whatever my questions are, I can let all of that stuff go and just live my life. I'm free to run a business and do whatever I want; go skydiving or climbing Mt. Everest.

Fighting Will

You can have whatever kind of existence you want, good or bad. The choice is up to you. What will you choose?

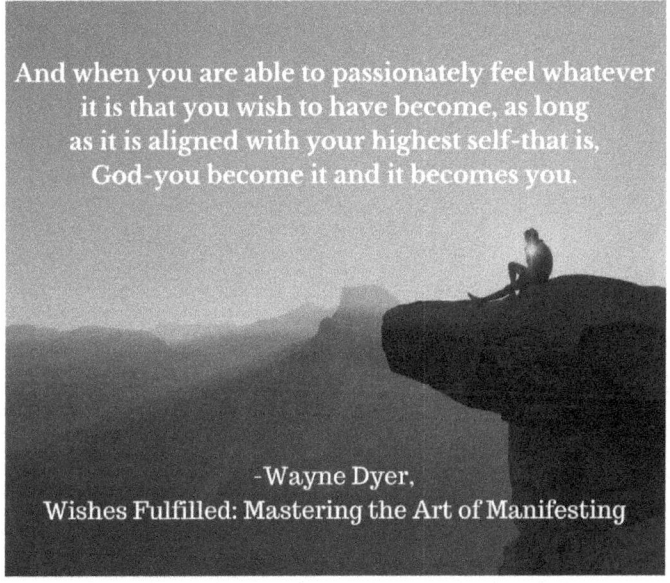

Luke Chichetto

ABOUT THE AUTHOR

Luke Chichetto was a former Strength and Conditioning Coach at the Tampa Bay Buccaneers & the Texas Rangers. He now runs his own company, Mobility RX Fitness http://mobilityrxfitness.com/, that helps improve mobility of the body and is a full comprehensive approach to fitness. He lives with his wife and three daughters in Clearwater, Florida. He is constantly working on new concepts to help the human body to perform physically the way they were designed.

Luke Chichetto

www.ingramcontent.com/pod-product-compliance
Lightning Source LLC
Chambersburg PA
CBHW071206160426
43196CB00011B/2208